BACK TO THE BARN

Also by James Forsyth

Other published works

Plays
EMMANUEL
THE OTHER HEART
HELOISE
ADELAISE
DEFIANT ISLAND
IF MY WINGS HEAL
SCREWTAPE
THE ROAD TO EMMAUS
Version of Rostand's CYRANO
Version of Ibsen's BRAND

Biography
TYRONE GUTHRIE

TV and Radio Plays

THE LAST JOURNEY
FOUR TRIUMPHANT
OLD MICMACK
THE ENGLISH BOY
THE PIER
TROG
WHEN THE SNOW LAY ROUND ABOUT
THE THRESHING FLOOR
THE BRONZE HORSE
LISEL
SEELKIE
CHRISTOPHE

BACK TO THE BARN

JAMES FORSYTH

Dear Charles at Olwyn – your copy.
with my love – a story you
know and took significant part in.

James.

20th May 1986.

GRAINLOFT BOOKS

ISBN 0 9511075 0 X

First published 1986 by Grainloft Books,
Grainloft, Ansty, Haywards Heath,
West Sussex RH17 5AG

Printed and bound in Great Britain
by Burgess & Son (Abingdon) Ltd.,
Abingdon, Oxfordshire.

ACKNOWLEDGEMENTS

For their help in the preparation of this book I have become deeply indebted to those close friends and staunch colleagues who have so encouraged, supported and assisted me: Stephanie Charman, John and Anne Evans, Michael Legat, Raymond Heavens, Jill Dutton and Christiane Carpenter.

There are those also who, by their years of willing and inspired work at the Barn, have made exceptional contribution to the spirit and success of its life as a theatre yet, by chance, have no mention in its story as told here; such as

Ian Blackwood and his whole family; Margaret Cattani and her whole family; Georgina Chilvers; Mary Clinton; Robert Cook; Mollie and Gerald Cox; Paul and Jean Davies and family; Paul and Karen Fisher; the Foster family; Rosemary Gee; Anne Graham-Evans; Daphne Grainger; Pat and Noelle Gwynne; Julia Harvey and family; Roger Heavens; Helen Hislop; Joan Hodge; the Hollinghurst family; Judith Howard and family; Edward Lawrence; Gillian Manly; Mary Marchant; Charles and Olwyn Moore; Don Nowell and family; Morwenna Nourse; Loveday Prior-Ward; Donald and Barbara Pasfield; Mark Ravenhill; Fred Rigby; Margaret and Clifford Riley; Margery Saw; John Stallwood and family; Jennie Sturrock; Ken and Betty Thomas; Margaret Walker, Susie, and family; Peggi Walls; Helen Wright and family.

In love and honour of
Louise

PROLOGUE

This is an improbable story but it is a true story; and a success story.

Once upon a, rather recent, time an isolated, deserted but beautiful old Barn, set in the heart of live Sussex farmland, became for only about ten years what may well have been one of the best 'theatres' in the Western World. That's the improbability.

Best, but not big; rough but real; and, though it was deeply satisfying to all concerned in the work it did, players, audience and hundreds others, I am not driven to write this book because of what it was so much as what its success implied. For this could be of real general interest both to all who are concerned with the Theatre Arts and the operation of community ventures. It was not 'planned' by any group. It simply *grew* because someone started working towards an imagined end and others heard and joined in the work. That its founders and the workers concerned formed no committees, had no rules, simply a Dedication to one aim, and had one Director (of that aim), this characterized the whole concern and was a significant truth in its success.

It was a success – even in cash – though it never had the size for, nor the intention of, making money; its chief expenditure being human effort and talent freely given in payment for the satisfaction of its aims. These aims all related to the Arts and the Art of Theatre; and they were targetted on the heart of Theatre, the play and players. In a technologically obsessed age it had by accident a Back to Nature sort of bias: rather back to human nature, where everything was manually operated, tangible; and immediate: nothing 'programmed', nothing press-button or remote-controlled. And because the Barn was its beginning it was Back to The Barn; not forward to the new architecture of technically planned theatres or the arid 'empty space' theatres of 'lab. theatre'. Which takes us to the Barn itself.

But two points to make first.

By official definition it was a 'private theatre' unable to throw its doors open to the public yet able, by its appeal, to serve a large local community. It was not a 'private theatre' for either of the two traditional reasons.

Its owners were not possessed of the 'private means' to do what was done, and at their leisure. The owners were already overworked and in the category of 'struggling artist-playwright and wife' with next to no capital. Nor was it planned to be elite and privately exclusive. It was anti-exclusive. It was local government regulations, in relation to the difficult access to its improbable location, which slapped the label 'Private' on it.

By definition it was 'amateur'. But it was under the professional direction of the playwright and was amateur in the proper sense; that all was done for love of Theatre: but *not* at all done 'for fun'. It was more creative than recreational and hard work – fully artistically disciplined – was there from the beginning.

The fact that players may depend on other daily work for the cash needed to pay bills does not necessarily deny them a professional commitment to their work in Theatre. A large section of the so-called Professional Theatre is better described as the Commercial Theatre of Show Business–where there need be no great *profession* to the art of Theatre. The best of the Barn artistes might be said to have become 'professed to Theatre'.

In an age when Theatre at its best, unless heavily subsidized by central governments, has been forced to become a sort of commercial commodity or a rather impoverished artistic product, it may be of concern that this small rural theatre did prove that, provided your economic mix is Talent, Time and a sweated Devotion to a high standard of performance on and off stage, there is really no need ever to be 'in the red' financially or for the work ever to be, in the apologetic sense, 'amateur'.

But ... in the beginning was the Barn. And when many of the poeple involved keep saying to me now, 'What was it? What was it that made it all effective; and so affected us? Was it the Barn itself or ...' Well the whole 'personality' of a building always does work for or against one; and the Barn did work *for* us.

THE BARN

There is a sort of occupational and gracious modesty about the architecture of spacious old big barns. They can have all the enduring graciousness of a great cathedral, without the pretentiousness of planned grace; spirit without spirituality. In a casual, workaday way, our Barn had that atmosphere. And we let that atmosphere at all times embrace the players and their play and also the audience played to. We never built 'a stage' nor any division between the static audience and the active players. It is simply observed fact that almost everybody coming first into the Barn gave a little gasp of surprise, half of which was the operation of the ancient business of human awe; the other half was pure pleasure. Yes – luckily for us the Barn itself was a large element in the success. But let's get to the facts which faced those involved.

The Barn is the largest of a group of Sussex farm buildings sitting seven hundred yards or so off the A272 where it turns to go West at the

Ansty Cross. On the ridge route of an old cross-country footpath the site of the buildings looks South across the Sussex weald to the back of the Downs at Ditchling Beacon. To the North it looks over the valley between it and Cuckfield: in which valley the River Adur, as a stream, begins its winding way towards the sea at Shoreham on the South coast. In that valley can be seen the roof of the old watermill down in what, before the days of the A272, was called 'the Cuckfield gorge'. The whole site is ancient and has produced evidence of habitation dating back to the 14th Century. Its yards and buildings proved rich in the relics of generations of farm use, such as bones of oxen, old cart wheels, old chains, rat traps, a sower's 'broadcasting box', old winnowing machines, horn corn measures etc, etc.

The group of buildings are: the Barn itself, with its double length of attached cowbyre on its North side; its outbuildings consisting of two vintage cowsheds of stone, brick, oak timbers and tile; a 20th century small stable of brick and tile; a brick cart shed (now a garage) and a small granary of brick, oak timber frame, tile and weather-boarding, which is of the same vintage and architectural merit as the Barn itself, and is now "Grainloft", the house of the author; finally "Old Place", the big old farmhouse from which our story begines and which once was probably a small manor, perhaps the millowner's house when the water wheel turned, perhaps the ironmaster's house when Sussex was a centre of the Tudor iron industry; for layers of ironstone run under the sandstone outcrop on which both Barn and Granary stand.

At the time our story begins, James Forsyth, the playwright, his wife Louise and two sons of a pre-war marriage had "Old Place" as their home. They were in the final phase of bringing the beloved old house up from a near derelict state where second son Richard had been bathed as a small boy in the deep old kitchen sink, the outside toilet was 18th century, housed in a garden gazebo, there was one water tap and the lighting was oil lamps; a down-to-earth start of a fortunate and loving occupancy. Somewhat Back to Nature. But, back to the Barn.

JAMES and LOUISE FORSYTH

invite you to a performance of

EMMANUEL

(a play for Christmas)

In the centuries old Sussex Barn at

O L D   P L A C E ,   A N S T Y

*(this is the first ever use of the barn as
a country theatre)*

*There will be 3 Performances
before an invited audience.*

SATURDAY,   9th DECEMBER   at   3.00 p.m.
and   7.00 p.m.

SUNDAY,   10th DECEMBER   at   5.00 p.m.

*******+*******

*It would be most helpful
if you would let us know
as soon as possible, which
performance you wish to
attend.*

R.S.V.P. to

Old Place, Ansty,
Haywards Heath,
Sussex.

Tel. 0444 - 3345

The first invitation 1972

xii

CHAPTER ONE

Nobody in our household had any intention of turning it into a *theatre*. Intentions theatrical never came into play until the thing had already started to grow; and intentions, when they did creep in, came in step by step to keep up with what was just naturally happening. In fact, so improbable was the whole thing in the beginning that maybe Nature or what some of us still call God did have an intention; though the siting of 'a theatre' down at the end of a narrow and pot-holed lane in the middle of agricultural Sussex would seem to be a God-awful choice, even if Nature beyond the mud was undeniably beautiful.

It just happened: one New Year's Eve. It started with what fashion in Theatre around that time called 'a happening' and without two vital ingredients on the spot I suppose it just would not have happened at all. One was the enduring nature of this big old stone and timber Barn with its fortunate attachment along its northern side of two spacious, solid and vintage cow-sheds. The second ingredient – leaven to this lovely lump as it were – was this playwright of considerable experience and with much of a reasonably distinguished career already behind him; but with things vital to the arts of theatre he had not yet fully put to the proof in plays written and unwritten. The character of the Barn was and is as I have said entirely benign, its spacious interior an invitation to the imagination and a dream of a place within which to communicate. The character of the playwright is a thing which I am in no position to be accurate about – it being mine. But I know for a certainty that this playwright had enough of a struggle to write the plays and convince people to risk producing them, without taking on the perilous business too of 'running a theatre'. In fact I had said at the time we became fortunate enough to be able to purchase the Barn that I wanted the money rather to be spent on efforts to get other unpublished plays into print. Ironically I had, many years before this, passionately persuaded my dear wife away from spending some inherited money in the chancy purchase of a redundant small cinema in the neighbouring town – to 'turn it into a theatre'. So – I didn't intend now to turn the barn into, . . . but forget intentions. We did *not* 'turn it into a theatre'. It might be said to have turned us back to what Theatre was all about in the beginning.

This was 1971. The farmer had no agricultural use for such a barn. So great new steel and concrete barns were built on another site within the extensive farmlands of which the fields around us were just a part. We bought it because we loved the building and we did not welcome anything or anyone unlovely in nature or function, coming in as a threat to the old farmhouse on whose restoration from near dereliction we had spent all our savings over many years.

Our story starts now, when we were on holiday at home and in the run-up to the New Year of 1972. Second son Richard, his fellow student friends and approved guests of his generation, had already had their sort of Christmas Party. The adult party occasion was to be on New Year's Eve. I made a resolution. But this was not a New Year's resolution relating to good behaviour in the year ahead. This was related to the one night: the night when the Old Year became the New. And for all the years we now had ahead of us this resolution dramatically changed the lives of my wife and myself.

The resolution was that we were not going to 'bring in the New Year' once again in front of the telly-box and with its embarrassing tartan on-screen capers of my fellow Scots. I was determined that this old year would be seen out and the New Year brought in with the ceremony and celebration due to it, by doing some sort of . . . well . . . How I was *not* going to bring in the New Year was clear. How I *was* was not clear. I did however clearly know *where* it was going to happen.

I put it to my wife. 'What do you think?'

'Very foolish,' she said; immediately and excusably linking the artist-playwright of the family to natural folly. And, with her compassionate mind as ever on the side of the persecuted and oppressed, she said, 'think of the cold – possibly damp too, *and* it will be dark.'

I wasn't shaken. '*That* is a *very dry* building. It was built to be so. As for the dark and the cold, they would be factors working *for*, not against me.'

It was the Barn, of course, we were talking of. My suggestion was to celebrate the arrival of the New Year in the old building so newly ours. But Louise remained true to form: gentle but firm. 'No. I'm against it. You've asked me and I'm telling you. You'll have several of our guests starting the New Year with pneumonia or worse. What do you mean – celebration? This was to be a *party*! – here, in the house, in the warmth.' She turned to go: to make a start on her domestic preparations for the impending party, New Year's Eve being very few evenings away. Her departing shot was 'Anyway there isn't time to do . . . well . . . whatever you wanted to do.'

With no precise sense of what I *was* going to do but no lack of determination now to do it, I wrapped up warm and went out on my own into the empty Barn. All I knew was that I wanted, in a meaningful and I hoped an entertaining way, to celebrate truly one of the festive occasions of everybody's year. And Celebration – it perhaps

2

should be noted now – was a root cause of all Drama – all the world's Theatre – in the beginning. But I would again point out that I wasn't intending to begin anything that would go beyond the stroke of midnight 1971; except perhaps 'Auld Lang Syne', sung by about forty frosty breathers. And – Lord! – I did *not* have much time. It also became painfully clear to me, as I stood alone out there in the Barn with December's chill breeze breathing through a thousand apertures in timbers and tiles, that the time of this celebratory entertainment would have to be limited to under a half hour's duration or my audience of guests would probably be into frostbite or hypothermia.

I set to work. As playwright professed to drama, I don't think that I ever worked harder to a deadline than in this bit of *wrighting*. (Because plays are *wrought* out of the stuff of the theatre arts, not *written*, except as record and recipe for the on-stage action.) What was wrought this time turned out to be a sort of twenty minute 'Masque on the Death and the Rebirth of the Year'. Academic theatre historians might finish up by listing it in the category of 'Primitive Assyrian-Style Resurrection Ritual Drama, related to fertility rites of old Sussex and modelled on elements of the Orpheus myth.'!

I wasn't modelling it on anything; except the ground I was standing on. And what was driving me was a vague determination to take people through the dark point of the dying year and into the hope and light ahead in the new.

It was still clear daylight outside and, for these moments of working the thing out on the spot, the only lighting I had in the deserted Barn was dramatic enough. It came streaming down from high up in the old wall of the southern gable; through two of the ancient 'owl holes'. These were the diamond shaped apertures in the medieval brickwork through which the local owls could come and go, to keep down the Barn's former population of rats. These would otherwise have lived too fat a life of leisure and sheltered procreation, taking toll of the grain harvest gathered in. When Louise was first walking on the deserted threshing floor that lay between the great West and the even greater East door she was 'dive bombed' by the silently swooping resident owl; a beautifully snowy sort of creature and no small bird but a very frightening 'sitting tenant'; except when he *was* sitting up there on a high cross-beam and snoring like a tramp asleep in the hay. There was now no hay or corn in the empty Barn and only the residual rat. But here I was as it were 'walking the boards', working out some kind of play. I could remember when I first had the advantage of doing this sort of foot-slogging professional preparation. That was in 'walking through' a play I was writing at the time when I was the post-war 'resident playwright' at the Old Vic (a play called *The Other Heart* which features dramatically in the end of the Barn's story.)

3

In the empty Barn I was not – as I had been at the Old Vic – actually walking 'the boards', except where I walked on the broad elm boards of the ancient 'deck' of the threshing floor which lay between the two great doors. I was, for the rest of the floor surface of the Barn, walking on impacted old straw and the accumulated agricultural detritus of generations of farming (three centuries at least). Apart from two small bays on the western side, the whole floor covered about 18 by 45 feet, in three areas not too different in extent; the northern and southern being separated by the middle area of the threshing-floor's 'deck'. Between the roughly level earthen area of the southern part and the wooden threshing floor there ran across the width of the Barn a four foot high wooden wall which I have always called the 'bulwark' – thinking of old wooden ships. Its ancient oak was time-worn to a polish, except where, in the ruts, the dust of ages lay. From the north edge of the threshing-floor there rose a steady slope which covered the whole northern area. This slope seemed to me to be made of the build-up of the old impacted hay, dung, droppings etc. But, from the first, it puzzled me . . . why should there be this slope up to the back of the Barn, where it then dropped down to a little oak-boarded door leading on and out into the two attached cow-byres?

Earlier that year I had in fact satisfied my curiosity about this slope. I had done a rather amateur but quite neat sort of archaeological 'dig'. Digging down into the tobacco-like layers of impacted hay etc, by about $1\frac{1}{2}$ to 2 feet I had struck stone, soft sandstone. A layer of honey-coloured sandstone was running parallel to the upper surface of the slope. It was the natural ridge of sandstone on which the foundation of the Barn and buildings stood; and from which the stone courses of the farm buildings were quarried.

My dig had finished up as a trench about $1\frac{1}{2}$ feet deep and 2 feet wide, 5 feet long. Its length lay north and south up the slope. The wide area of the slope itself faced across the threshing floor, to the southern flat area where now I knew my 'audience' would stand beyond the 'bulwark'. I now was looking down into a sort of 'grave'; very suitable as a setting for the grave-digger scene from *Hamlet*. But, being mad more north than north-north-west, I uttered a cry more Scottish than Danish but meaning in any language 'Eureka'! The barn owl, had he been up there on his high roof-beam, would have awakened to see the shaft of highly dramatic light falling across this 'grave' and would have heard the crazy human creature below emphatically say, *'This is where we'll bury the Old Year!'* I still didn't know *what* I was saying, just *why*; but nobody could say, could they, that our approach to our theatre wasn't down to earth?

I went on from this point, plotting, pacing, muttering and noting down in an excited sort of shorthand, eg:

'fresh and golden bale of straw to be placed at head of grave – grave of the Year . . . as sort of altar'. From this grave I needed the stage space – and I had it – the space to walk out from the back of the Barn a diminishing zig-zag. Along this the King – King of Day, symbol of all Light and Warmth of the World would pursue a diminishing course to end up by dying down into the grave. 'Have to be choreographed – rhythmic movement – to rhythmic speech . . . also zig-zag music. *Music*? What music? Think later, but wife's niece's daughter plays well enough on recorder. Don't hide her. No illusion. Sit her on other bale of hay – up-stage right. Costume? Costumes utterly simple – single colours? and masks! Masks?' Well, one couldn't expect the human face – even with stylized make-up – to register the length of a long Barn dimly lit. 'Light! What lighting' . . . Well . . .

Under pressure of time and with devotion to the one end of meaningful and dramatic Celebration, a very non-technological production began to take shape; literally from the ground up. Starting from that discovered 'grave' of the year and that proposed straw 'altar' of its resurrection, I found myself behaving, in a crude but creative way, like the priest/playmakers who had wrought the old dramatic rituals now mostly lost in the source areas of all the world's Drama. Seriously . . . by accident, but for the same reason – to celebrate a crisis in the cycle of the year (probably the dark one which most primitive folk feared) – and to touch people today at the roots of experience common to us all – I was 'wrighting', (and just barely writing down) what Drama was designed to do in the beginning.

For players, I knew there would be three gifted young professionals among our party guests; one to become a distinguished player of the Royal Shakespeare Company and now noticeably busy on film and T.V., Nickolas Grace. Nick could be counted on to be bullied into playing King of Day (he could choreograph movement also). The other two both came from the Shakespeare Festival Theatre, Ontario, and while in London had been made a sort of theatrical niece and nephew to Louise and me by our great friend, and my mentor in Theatre, Tyrone Guthrie. One of them, Liza Hagon, could be coaxed to play Daughter of Day and Night.

When it became obvious that Father's 'celebration' was to be a sort of play it needed no great persuasion to get student son Richard to play the villain of the piece, The Prince of Darkness. Louise, my modest mentor in all things, might be chivvied out of shyness to play Queen of the Night, only if limited to one line, up-stage, in shadow, masked. We had the human resources necessary.

As for Technical Equipment, Props, Lights, etc, their crude nature makes the point for me that it requires no sophisticated equipment at all to achieve powerfully moving and meaningful effect in Theatre:

5

For SOUND equipment: 1) A *recorder* played by beautiful young daughter of my wife's niece with a tune composed by her to the following specification: 'Zig-zag theme, Elizabeth, to go along with The King of Day as he zig-zags towards the grave, like this; as it, and he, grows weaker all the way.'

2) *A child's tambourine* that had lost its skin (the tambourine, not the child).

For LIGHTING: 1) *A car inspection light* and longish lead. (The sort of thing with which you look under the bonnet identifying trouble on a dark, wet night on the soft shoulder of a motorway.) This with an amber bulb to be set in a short section of a half glazed drain pipe stood upright at the foot of the slope. This should cast a warm glow over the cold 'grave' and on and up to the golden fresh bale of straw at its head. A sort of first generation footlight, but electric.

2) *An anglepoise desk lamp*; also with a longish lead, to throw a bit of cold directional light up along the course of the 'zig-zag'.

3) *A borrowed motor showroom flood*, strapped up, at some peril, owl-high on one of the great cross-beams of the Barn roof. (Use related to picnic basket set below in the 'grave', but top-secret till performance.)

For COSTUME: 1) Shoulder-to-shin length *panels of cloth of pure colours* almost shoulder width and attached at the upper end to some shoulder width batons of bamboo. These would be held over the fronts of their bodies by the player's left hand.

2) Held in the player's right hand would be *the mask*: a shallow wooden seed box nailed at the back to a vertical baton of bamboo and on its front, on tough paper pasted upon the flat of the box, a simplified, stylized visage of the character (King of Day, Queen of Night, Daughter of Day and Night). These were drawn with broad felt pen (and tested on the spot for range and readability). (See page xi.) The Prince of Darkness had the encouraging privilege of a professional theatrical mask. This looked like a grey death mask but was in fact the plague mask of Catherine de Vausselles of *The Other Heart* a relic from an American production of that play.

For SPECIAL PROPS: 1) *A Cloth of the Earth* (of hessian) large enough to cover the area of the open grave.

2) *A Cloth of the Frost* (made of a large old bedsheet) the same size as the above and frosted with silvery sequins. Both cloths secured, like great banners, to eight feet long rough-cut bean poles.

3) *A large old ship's bell*, transferred from its usual bracket outside our back door, to hang in the cowshed just outside the little north door into the Barn. (North End, Up-Stage end). *And* then – the mystery bit of equipment.

4) *A shallow wicker picnic basket* able to be accommodated in the grave along with two persons. No picnic this!

New Year's Eve arrived. By the time the cars of the early party guests were trundling down between frozen fields – down our long and pot-holed lane; trundling towards the heart of rural Sussex and a warm welcome in a warm house with log fires burning, there were scripts of a kind ready. These were just recipes for action with essential rhythmic dialogue. There was also the text of a short Prologue to be spoken by myself as acting host to the guest audience. With some wicked persuasion on my part and much good will on theirs, I had my cast of four quicker into action than Hamlet's lot of travelling players at Elsinore. Rehearsal was intensive, out there in the remaining daylight hours of the great old Barn. With no union restriction applicable, the players and I could be double-purpose participants, pressing switches, setting props etc. There was no need of stage-hands where the 'unit set' was limited to two bales of hay, a length of unmarked zig-zag on the ground, and the props were just the Cloths of the Earth and Frost and, of course, that mystery wicker-work picnic basket.

But – to the event. Having rehearsed the little company and then fearing that our audience might never get to us if the night was damp and the going was the sort of Sussex mud that can bog down a strong tractor even on a frosty surface, we took to work laying a narrow walkway of straw. We laid this from the front door of the house round into and across the walled barnyard which is created by the angle of the Barn and the two long cowsheds. Going in through the cowsheds and out onto the west side of the Barn we laid again the straw-way, going south and close to the building, then on up to a small door in the south Bay. This door led straight into the earth floor area to the south of the threshing floor behind the 'bulwark', where the audience would stand (for 20 perishing minutes at the maximum).

Perishing, but not damp, for the night turned out to be cold as corrupt charity and the ground was frosted crisp but firm. Stars were in the sky. Towards the end of the party in the house, eats, drinks and seasonable chatter having gone with a swing, my nervous wife slipped out to her undisclosed but thespian duties in the Barn; still with pessimism about the celebration to come: 'They *can't* stay long out there. It's *bitterly* cold'. I dressed myself up, as furlined and warm booted as a Tolstoyan mujik, and to the guests in the house – (about forty-five) who were now gathered within the warmth of the great old log fire in the main room, I gave this Invitation – plus Instruction.

'Ladies and gentlemen! – including the Doctor! – in half an hour's time will you please wrap yourselves up super warm and be ready to come out into the night with me'. 'Wow! Why?' Laughter and no answer from me. '*And* bring with you some robust drinking receptacle, like a mug or jam jar or such'. More puzzlement and giggling 'and please pick up on your

7

way a handful of something, as an inoffensive missile with which to pelt the Old Year when we see him out. Thank you!'

Evading questions I nipped out to the dark Barn to check that my 'beginners' were in position and ready; and that, now that it was dark, a winding 'flare path' of small storm lanterns was lit along the length of the strawpath to the Barn. It was starry clear, when I led the happy, noisy yet not unapprehensive, procession of guests out into the chill night and along the prepared straw-way. As I led this processional serpent of bemused souls through the night an outside observer might have been excused for thinking that here was some bit of revived primitive ritual on the move. In one hand I carried a storm lantern and in the other a small cowbell which I rang at regular intervals along the route. But this bell in the night had no ritual significance. It was for the purely practical purpose of letting the players in the dark of the Barn know exactly where their audience was; as it wound its way towards them.

But it was rather like a presiding priest that I led them through the frosty yard. Gusts of laughter, and grumbling mutters too, came out into the night in frosty breaths as I led them on into the dark cowsheds. I led them along its unlit length, my little lantern their only light on the way, then out into the starry night again, then turning south along the straw-way hugging the west wall of the Barn; till they didn't know what the devil of a dance they were being led; or to where: certainly not to what. In through the little door of the south bay they followed me into the Barn; to find themselves standing on what felt like dry earth with, above and around their heads, a great unknown and dark spaciousness. Leaving them there like a flock of huddled sheep whose shepherd was deserting them, I climbed the 'bulwark', crossed the threshing floor, up the slope, past the invisible Prince of Darkness, flattened now like a great bat against the boarding of the east wall. Then, continuing up the slope I – and the one light in the place, my little storm lantern – disappeared through the little door which led into the cowsheds. The audience were left apparently deserted and in the utter and cold dark, with no sound except a sigh or two of the night wind breathing through the innumerable apertures of this great wooden tent.

I am told that some of the more townee guests were actually scared. For this was a new experience to them of primitive non-urban darkness. The darkness persisted until the silence was broken by the entirely inexpert but utterly sweet playing of the recorder up at the North-End of their darkness. Surreptitiously the Prince of Darkness, doing double duty as electrics operator, pressed a switch and a warm amber glow spread up and onto the golden bale of straw on the breast of the slope. As 'mine host' I then came out and forward into the glow, and spoke a welcoming prologue. To those gathered where the grain used to be gathered it reminded them in a bit of rough-hewn poetry of the use of the Barn for the storing of the harvest and the theme was struck of how the dark and cold must come and the seed must seem to die so that the new plant may grow.

As I retired the music took up its 'zig-zag' theme and a directional shaft of light was thrown up-stage and on to the young recorder player seated on her bale of straw. And, as little Elizabeth played, up-stage of her came out on to the slope the masked and gold robed King of Day. Moving in rhythm and speaking to the beat of the music he was pursued by the multi-robed (three super-imposed panels of red, gold and green) Daughter of Day and Night. And, as the King moved to the music, she, anxious at his failing strength, questioned him. He answered her – question followed by response in rhythm – as he continued on his obviously diminishing course, towards the open grave. There he sank down into the dark of the grave and out of sight. On this the Prince of Darkness swept off the wall, swept up his great hessian banner of the Cloth of the Earth, and brought it down over the gaping grave, burying the King of Day. Then the Queen of Night, in the shadows by the north and wooden wall, bemoaned the death of all warmth and all light. But, being a more militant female, the Daughter of Day and Night then started her one-person protest. This mustn't be! Warmth and Light cannot be allowed to die. So – like a female Orpheus on the way to the Underworld – she, musically and rhythmically, set out on *her* zig-zag course to the grave. Her intent was to rescue her father. At each point of her zig-zag progress the Prince of Darkness stepped out and challenged her.

eg (roughly from memory):

PRINCE OF DARKNESS
What do you want?

DAUGHTER OF DAY
The warmth of the sun.

PRINCE OF DARKNESS
Then give me the *red* robe; and come on.

(He stripped the panel of red from her front and draped it over the straw bale 'altar'. She then went on another zig-zag nearer the grave; and again was challenged).

PRINCE OF DARKNESS
What do you seek?

DAUGHTER OF DAY
The gold of the dawn.

9

PRINCE OF DARKNESS
Then give me the *gold* robe; and come on.

(The gold panel of cloth stripped from her body and laid on the 'altar', by the red. She moves again, close to the edge of the Earth Cloth covering the grave.)

PRINCE OF DARKNESS
What do you hope for Daughter of Day?

DAUGHTER OF DAY
The first sprig of May; the green of the Spring.

PRINCE OF DARKNESS
Then give me the *green* robe; (whipping it off) and you are in the ring of encircling Winter.

(Taking up the banner of the Earth and swinging it away from the grave).

As he swung the great hessian banner of the Cloth of the Earth up and round in the cold air of the Barn she looked down, saw the King in the grave, stepped down into it and the Prince of Darkness brought the sweep of hessian down to fall over her, trapping her like a bird; burying her also in the grave. Then with a bit of poetic triumph he swung into play the banner with the Cloth of Frost and laid this on top of the Cloth of the Earth. The warm light died down. And to the huddled, very human, audience, the Prince of Darkness sang out of his death mask into the frosty air an old Sussex folk song about the hard and cold of the year; a mocking song sung over the grave with its Earth cover and Frost cover. At its end the whole Barn went dark. The music stopped. There was silence.

This was, for the audience in its darkness, the Dark of the Year. At which point Nature actually supplied for us an inspired unsought Sound Effect: a whisper of winter wind stole through the Barn like a chill shudder. Then, out of the darkness came a sound, a shivering little tinkle of the child's tambourine (shaken by me in the dark opening of the little door to the cowshed). This was followed by a statement of doubt by the Prince *in* Darkness: 'Something stirs frost cannot chill'. Then a further metallic shiver of sound. 'Something lives I cannot kill'. It was then that, with full relish in the moment, I bellowed out into the specious darkness of the Barn:

'The Year that was old is becoming new!
The Love at the heart of Creation drives through
the darkest night!!'

10

And I bashed out a loud peal on the old ship's bell and, praying hard that the uncertain wiring would work, pressed a small switch on the lead that led up to the borrowed floodlight.

Suddenly the great upper beams and upper roof areas of the Barn were suffused with light; and down below, out of the grave, fluttered *two white doves!* Gasp from the audience as they flew out on to the red, gold and green 'robes' lying on the bale of straw, then flew up, on and up to the great cross beam and the light above. And out of the grave in his gold robe rose up the King of Day and his laughing Daughter. The other lights were switched on under cover of the audience's surprise and the cast together with me turned on him and started to chase the Prince of Darkness round the Barn. As he came round on the 'deck' before the audience they pelted him from behind the old 'bulwark' with straw, dung etc. Finally we chased him up the slope and out through the little open door to the dark cowshed. As I slammed shut the little door we had 'seen out' the 'Spirit of Cold and Dark of the Old Year'. And – The Queen of the Night, who had disappeared in the earlier darkness reappeared to welcome applause as my warm-hearted wife, coming down the slope to the audience carrying before her a big steaming bowl of hot punch. They got out their mugs, glasses etc and she filled them up. The Prince of Darkness, unmasked as my smiling son, pressed the 'On' switch of a large transistor radio we had pre-set on a low beam by the east wall and with only seconds 'off-cue', Big Ben rang out into the Barn, from Westminster, London, the chimes of midnight 1971.

That was it. The thrill was obvious, the warmth of their appreciation had nothing to do with degrees of temperature and we had difficulty getting our guests to quit the Barn for the physical warmth of the house. These were they who would protest or die of pneumonia! They flooded on to the threshing floor and burst into enthusiastic comment.

A 'total surprise' and 'the quality', 'so simple, so rough but such quality'. '*and* the doves!' 'How did you . . . ?' Well, I had rehearsed another two of our doves the day before (and had had as much difficulty afterwards in getting them down and out of the building as getting the audience now back to the house.) But I had seen then for certain that they would fly up towards the source of light.

The two white beauties cast for the role 'on the night' were, on the previous night, taken by me from their loft in the old house, and put into the wicker basket. This, on the day, was taken out to the Barn and planted in the bottom of 'the grave'. All that the adept King of Day had to do – though squeezed in with his daughter as well – was to withdraw a peg to release the lid and on the stroke of the bell push back the cloths of Earth and Frost and out the doves fluttered and up they flew;

11

beautiful in their delicate whiteness and lightness by contrast to the heavy darkness before.

From our satisfied and surprised audience the most repeated comments were 'total surprise', '– but the quality of it all' and 'Do more'. When Louise asked her cousin's son to be sure to tell his mother how it was, Johnny – a Friend of Covent Garden and an opera addict whose standard of the stage arts was of top quality – said, 'Sorry. I can't. No. I couldn't convey what happened here tonight – but . . . ' and again, '*Do more*'. Even then there was no sense of having landed ourselves with a *theatre*; perhaps an obligation simply to celebrate in the Barn again such a seasonal event.

But we all went back into the old house with a profound sense of truly having 'brought in' the New Year of 1972.

If I have dealt in considerable detail with this very small-scale dramatic event in a way that I cannot afford to do with quite major productions to follow, it is because the implications in this beginning – as with the whole operation of the Barn as theatre – were perhaps even more important than the event. Size, or scale, is of secondary importance. Almighty in its importance was the *sort* of satisfaction of this ad hoc (mostly non-theatrical) audience. We had seemed to satisfy, by the nature of what we had done, a real need, using *very* local resources. Should we 'do more'?

Michael Legat and Louise Potter as Joseph and Mary in *Emmanuel*

12

CHAPTER TWO

We were now into 1972. Even if we had wanted to respond to the demand 'Do more' it hardly seemed possible in the year ahead. We both had too much to do, in work that we hoped would stem our diminishment towards a sort of financial grave. Our reserve fund in a building society was fading away. And if you are freelance with no regular arrival of any salary or final pension other than the national, you do need some reserve.

For the four previous years we had run, from a small hotel in Kensington, an overseas programme in Drama and English for students of Tufts University (of Medford, Massachusetts). Louise as Administrative Executive – in which field she was a professional genius – and I as Director Lecturer – in which field I was an amateur eccentric. It was fascinating; not least because we were taking young and talented Americans through the years of Student Protest and in a very old-fashioned British way. It had been lucrative. *But* I had little time to write. Louise had too little time at home and we too often passed each other – like the two fishes on our shared zodiacal sign – going in opposite directions; one on the 'up', one on the 'down' Brighton line.

We had resigned the year before; giving up two good dollar salaries. And that was the year we acquired an off-stage sound which became as permanent a part of the Barn's atmosphere as the cooing of some of our doves who deserted their loft for highrise living under the eaves above the owl holes of the Barn's south gable. This off-stage sound was the bleat of a sheep called 'Pax'. The motto of Tufts University is 'Pax et Lux' and that winter we had christened two orphaned twin lambs we'd adopted as 'Pax' and 'Lux'. 'Lux', the light, went out some years ago, but 'Pax' for peace can still supply that off-stage sound which penetrated the old wooden walls and was familiar to the Barn audience.

Despite breadwinning necessities – let's confess – I did now very much want to see if the Barn really had the possibility of being a natural sort of playhouse. The only true test of this would be to produce a whole play, in it as it stood.

By the Summer of that year – 1972 – we had privately decided what to do – a play suggested by Louise as both suitable to the Barn setting and fitting in too with my love of celebration of a festive occasion. We couldn't do anything earlier anyway, so it had better be a play for Christmas.

Testing the Barn fully and testing a full audience too, we would produce *Emmanuel* my 'nativity' play. This is in fact a full-length

13

suspense drama on the birth of the child Christ told like a Judean folk-drama. Again it would be 'in the bleak mid-winter', no heating; some hired lighting, company part-professional; costumes? . . . Well, let's leave the details till later.

During that Summer the family and relatives helped us get rid of some of the mud in the approaches; also to lay some hardcore; while in the cowsheds all the encrustation of dry dung was shovelled out. But it was while I was shovelling out stuff from the floor of the south end of the Barn, where the audience would be somehow seated, that the first helper outside the family arrived.

This help came unsought and was typical of how the whole thing grew. The neighbour who with his wife runs the store and sub-post office at the road end of the lane heard activity in the Barn, looked in and saw me shovelling. Cliff Smith asked for another shovel, rolled up his sleeves and joined me. And, he was a former CSM in the Guards, and wartime recruitment had once made me an Acting Unpaid Corporal in the Scots Guards; so pace and progress picked up.

Within a week my co-shoveller was saying to other locals, 'We're building a theatre down there.' Which claim was in the field of clairvoyance while we were still in the realms of faith and hope. But, soon the company of co-operators on *Emmanuel* – players and pro-duction team – had on its books, two carpenters, a butcher, a brewery official, a civil servant, a composer, two students, a bank clerk, a management consultant, a nationally known humorist, a professional actor and two trained drama students; not to mention a farm-worker's wife, the daughter of a West End manager and a considerable collection of lady helpers. And we weren't 'building a theatre'. Nobody was deciding yet what we were doing; except doing a play for Christmas in the Forsyths' Barn.

By September we had privately made our plans. By October we had gathered a sort of company. With production workers and players we all gathered together in the big room of the old house – by the same log fire from which I had summoned and led the first 'audience' forth – and we held a reading of the whole play (later cut to a compassionate length for the audience, of two periods of 35 minutes; with one interval for thawing out). The entry in our desk diary of that day of the reading says.

> 'Amazing response to *Emmanuel* for the Barn. Play almost fully cast . . . two marvellous meetings. *We have started something.*'

By November we sent out a local appeal to the village and rural community for extra hands to help. And by the same month Louise and her minions got out an Invitation (see illustration). The drawing of the little black lamb on this was done from the actual prop black lamb, called in the play 'Emmanuel', and who had featured in the English first ever production in 1951 and in 1960 had crossed the Atlantic to appear in the New York Off-Broadway production. There the play did well enough to steal, in the Winter of 1960, the New York Times First Night notice from *Camelot*, which opened on the same night. We reckoned we had a lucky mascot. But, in rehearsal we ran into our first crisis.

By late November, or early December a friendly but concerned Council Officer tapped me on the shoulder to say, 'You are breaking the law, you know.' With the accumulation of guilt gained from a life of wayward non-conformity, I thought, 'My God, what have I done now?' I had in fact invited to a performance, under a roof owned by me, possibly a hundred souls from far and wide and acceptances had rolled in. 'You need a licence. You'd better get one'. (If 'they' – the Council – would give it to me!) 'But I can't! I mean there isn't time.' 'Fire precautions – sanitary arrangements – should be inspected.' Time! There just wasn't time now. 'Well . . . ' There was no threat, just a friendly warning. I decided there and then, with the paranoiac intensity of any producer on the run up to Dress Rehearsal, that this 'crime' was my personal responsibility and I was prepared to go to jail after the event rather than do anything before the event to risk it not taking place at all. With our own fully practical fire precautions and adequate though primitive sanitary arrangements we went ahead; unlicensed.

We did our three performances to three 'houses' of an average audience of a hundred, all of whom left the Barn alive, and in a state of enthralled satisfaction. The 'appreciation', put into the collecting baskets of two players nightly left us with a profit of £33 and fourpence 'for future production'. Now we had not just 'started something', we now had to go through with it. And I wasn't in jail! (Louise just making tactful enquiries as to how we could get a licence.) No, I wasn't in jail, I was in bliss; after that Last Night. And waking up in the great old 'Bishop's Bed' (from whose oak legs we had once sawn off six inches so that the old dog could still lollop on to the foot of it in the morning) I awoke to the amazing realisation '*We have a theatre in our own backyard!*'

It was in a reaction of somewhat solemn consideration – about the responsibilities arising now – that the next highly critical thing happened. Responsibilities of finding the way forward arose; for not only myself but all those who would inevitably be involved in that creative jungle The Theatre. Yes – even in our lovely neck of the woods this was Theatre. I began to think of some simple Guiding Principles which would keep the best artistic aims clear amid all the complexities of personal hopes, ambitions, misunderstandings that can bedevil any theatrical venture. And by the time we had returned our £13 worth of hired lighting and put the Sound tape of Herod's Night trumpets to sleep, and the tape recorder in out of harm's way, it happened.

On a morning walk with the dog, down the field path that gets the southern sun, I thought up as I walked, a sort of dedication for the Barn – as theatre. It would perhaps be best to have not rules and regulations but some general convictions which we could be committed to. There was no pondering on it. It was simply set down on return to the house. The time the dog fed was long enough to draft it. On 29th December – after we'd had a reunion in the house of most of those who had taken part in *Emmanuel* I took them out into the evening, into the Barn, and, standing by the bales of hay where our Joseph had brought his Mary to rest after that journey. I read out this:

It is in the conviction that resolutions truly made are very persistent in what we consequently do, that we, Louise and I, make this –

DEDICATION

We believe that Love is the power at the heart of Creation.

We believe that true Art can provide a nourishment for a hunger which the whole of humanity has.

Therefore, whatever the fads or fashions of the time, we are resolved to do, in this Barn, works in the various Arts which genuinely contain real nourishment and generate true love; and we are resolved to deny this lovely old building to works and people whose spirit is – trivially or profoundly – destructive.

So, in respect of the level of Art and craftsmanship which created this lovely old Barn, may all who are prepared to join us in the spirit of this Dedication, give and receive the opportunity, within this place, of working creatively together. And may it always be the very best that we can do in all the Arts of Theatre; in Sound, Light, Sight and Touch.

Louise and I signed it on the 'table top' of the bales of hay and – with the cold air still frosting our breaths – the others came and added their signatures.

Now we *had* started something. We could hardly go back after this. For better or worse; the Barn *was* becoming a sort of theatre.

CHAPTER THREE

This has been the highly personal account of the beginning which it was bound to be; the whole thing having started from hearth and home, and from a purely personal resolution.

But, though in the histories of theatres and theatre companies it has seldom been a disadvantage to have as driving force one person's formative vision, it is in the nature of the composite art of theatre that it must involve and evoke the talents of many persons to bring its work to full fruition. When the many talents in the separate arts and crafts of theatre *are* allowed to contribute and *are* coaxed, nursed and bullied towards the one end, in the service of the play, then Theatre is the richest and most potent art form in the world. By the same token – of its several essential contributors – it is capable of tearing itself to pieces and producing the most pathetic of flops of even the best of plays; where there is no direction taken and no single end sought.

So – whatever the benefits to the project of a devoted tyrant as director – let me now try to draw back a bit from what happened so much on my own doorstep and so close to my heart. Let me treat the two inevitably key figures in the story – my wife and myself – as Louise and James and as objectively as possible describe how all the others came in and how our Barn grew to become the theatre it did. For grow, it did.

It is a point to keep hold of, that it was not so much 'planned' as *grew*. From the essential requirements of each production, undertaken as we faced its needs, it grew to become a fully effective playhouse. Necessity *was* the Mother of Invention at the Barn and most needs in costume, props, setting etc were invented from material more or less on the spot: native to our location.

Perhaps, by this kind of origination so concentrated on the Barn and its close environment, we did stumble into something like the cultural potency of a primitive 'native' village, with its severely local resources mobilised to meet the needs of a folk festival. Our events did tend to feel, both in their preparation and performance like a one-off celebration or mini-festival.

Three examples of such use of local resources may clarify:

1) The use of a local source of rough *hessian*, coming up on page 19; 2) the need for a certain character to props and setting for an old Chinese play satisfied by a harvesting of *bamboo* which grew in the mud by the millpond; and 3) when a crude Nativity 'babe' for a manger

made of local willow lath was needed and which was supposed to be in – in this particular Christmas celebration play – the product of the simpleton Franciscan, Brother Juniper, then the maker of this prop, James, looked around the Barn yards. In the old woodshed he found a rough billet of wood – roughly baby size – chose the sort of instrument Juniper would have chosen, a primitive old cleaver, and, as if in the character, he sat by the chopping block in the sun, with doves fluttering up from the grass where the chippings fell, and chipped the block of wood into a sort of crude doll which then he swaddled in some sacking from an old wool sack. On-stage in the Barn it worked a treat. Art Verité of primitive potency! and *expensive*; but only in time and thought taken.

Not much was brought in or bought in and the nature of the building, as theatre, grew as certain requirements of a particular production (in say staging, lighting, seating) proved to be worth keeping: for example the players' gallery for *The Festival of the Four*; the old signal box lighting set for *She Stoops to Conquer*; and of course the 'Auditorium' for *Emmanuel*. So what did this first production of a full play bring into being that stuck, as part of the growing theatre?

It perhaps gives a sense of the primitive and rural nature of this unheated production in the heart of winter if I tell you how narrowly the most innocent child of all in the Massacre of the Innocents was nearly Victim number one. We were all in various degrees victims of the cold, and one player maintained that he never regained feeling in his feet till, with car heater full on, he was just short of Croydon. During those frozen rehearsals on the run up to Christmas this headline could have been carried by the local press: MICE EAT CHRIST-CHILD! To achieve the proper limp weight for the babe asleep in Mary's arms, Louise had his cotton form stuffed with a mixture of lentils and millet. And one night, weary props had forgotten to put away 'the babe' in the old steel cupboard in the cowsheds backstage. With owl holes now glazed to keep out the winter wind there were no owls on hand to choose meat above cereals, and save the Redeemer from the rodents! A respectful refill was necessary; more millet; more child-care.

The requirements for settings of the first play were utterly simple. Apart from a manger of local willow, bales of straw, some hessian screening of the upstage entrance from the stable, a throne for Herod and an old cowshed door re-hung so that it squeaked (to echo a line in the script) the Barn playing-area as it stood, soil, sandstone and oak was 'a natural' for a nativity play. It was the requirement for seating the audience which led to a monument of local invention and a permanent feature of the Barn as theatre:

THE AUDITORIUM

One of the first of the volunteer workers at the Barn was John Lower, carpenter. He was a master carpenter of the local builders whom the Forsyths had used in all the restoration work on Old Place. At the time when the Barn and its buildings had been acquired the same builders had been brought in to do the limited work to make the massive timber structure of the Barn safe and sound; also to put in a new, but old oak, little door in place of the flimsy one where the first ever 'audience' had been herded in on New Year's Eve, 71/72.

So, John was already familiar with the Barn; but the world of Theatre was foreign territory to him. However, he was more than intrigued by what 'old James was adoing down there' (the 'old' being more affection than age). And he had a warm regard for the 'Clerk o' Works', as Louise had been nick-named during the restoration work at Old Place; restoration being her forte. She had in fact, sixteen happy years of marriage ago, 'restored' James to full vitality, following his ruinations marital and financial resulting from rash youth and cruel war, and had dug up in the process the historic motto of the Forsyth clan crest, 'Instaurator Ruinae'; translated – more or less – as 'the restorer of ruins'. James openly declared himself a ruin restored.

John heard him talk of the need to seat the audience for the Christmas play; talk of some shallow rostrum to set borrowed chairs upon; perhaps two levels of rostrum; on the earth floor to the south of the old 'bulwark'.

Already John's roving eye had enriched the proposed Christmas production by acres of hessian; tough material of a primitive but good quality and of a nature that was in complete harmony with the nature both of the Barn and the nativity story. It enriched the production and ruined Louise's washing machine! The hessian hadn't quite 'fallen off the back of a lorry' but had been spotted by John as abandoned in great quantity by the nearby main London-Brighton road after the completion of the new flyover. It was impregnated with cement! Louise's restoration of its splendid textured weave asked too much of ageing washing machine. But – almost all of the painted costume and scenic elements of *Emmanuel* were of lovely weathered hessian.

From this gifted craftsman with the crafty smile and the very alert roving eye James, one night, received a telephone call in the old house.

'James? . . . John . . . ' characteristic long pause to precede considered statement . . . then the deep Sussex yeoman voice.

'About this Seating . . . ' (pause) 'If I got you up noine foot at the back . . . '

'What are you talking about, John? . . . '

19

He was talking about a raked auditorium; though he would never have used that word from the foreign world of Theatre. When however an 'auditorium' was mentioned – by them as should ought to know – it acquired a sort of magical propriety and importance and John never again talked of building seating but of making an Auditorium.

'Well . . . I got some timber around and I've got a nodding acquaintance, you know, with an unemployed telephone pole, besides there's a tree in the wood back of the house has to come down. And the boss would let you have plenty scaffolding boards over the Christmas holidays, to give seating for people. And – '
'John, wait, Did you say *nine* feet? . . .
Call you back right away.'

And right away James left his writing desk and Act Three of a play on the Buonaparte family. He grabbed a torch, went out, got a long haystack ladder and went on into the empty Barn. Putting the ladder up against the south wall and between the two owl hole windows he went – backwards – up the ladder rung by rung till the seat of his trousers was roughly the nine feet up. Looking down northwards and sweeping it with the beam of the big torch, he scanned the whole slope, the upstage level and the deck of the down-stage threshing floor: the whole playing area north of the bulwark lying before him below.

If it wasn't it should have been the moment he decided he was deceiving himself in saying that this production was just to be a test of whether the Barn was a potential playhouse. At this elevated position of the audiences' point of view he was so emotionally thrilled that he might well have lost his footing, fallen off and been hospitalised for the whole period of the production. But he got down and back to the telephone in record time:

'John . . . ' uncharacteristic long pause for James, to get breath back.
'Yeah? . . . '
'If you *can* get me up nine feet at the back, I can promise you *wonders*.'

These were the immodest and actual words. But he meant it; and it meant more than a one-off commitment. 'Okay-doke!' was the irreverent but solemn reply as John moved towards his dream of Auditorium. Yet – one dark night, after weeks of nights and week-ends of work, John's rustic dream of classical success had to be scrapped.

From rash drawings of James and with a scratch crew, of Graham, his apprentice, Graham's father, the butcher, Bob Driver, the shepherd who yearly sheared our pet sheep and other stalwart local volunteers, John had got his basic framework as high as the promised nine feet when expert opinion visited the site, in the person of the husband of Louise's niece. He had earlier supervised and sweated on new hardcore approaches to the Barn, and was a very accomplished civil engineer.

'For God's sake stop!' Alec more or less said. So, James nervously asked John and his devoted gang to stop, down tools, and listen. Bob Driver, perched on top of half an orphanned telephone pole, in the cold, listened, tool in hand.

To let the Auditorium structure rest in anyway on the structural shell of the Barn itself, when one hoped that the seating might be carrying at any one time over a hundred highly mobile and applauding souls; also when the basic structure of the seating now in construction could not be guaranteed to be utterly rigid! – this was courting off-stage tragedy. The Auditorium *must* be free-standing from the walls and be completely rigid.

'You mean take this all down?'
'Yes, John. Sorry'. There was a chill moment of silent dejection; then, 'Take it away boys, we're starting again'.

It was a hard night. Louise brought the disheartened crew beer for some, steaming coffee for others. Alec went home to draw up proper plans, while James covered his shame, at having led John on, by committing considerable Forsyth cash to the purchase of all the necessary new timber, bolts etc; from which to make the monumentally rigid and free-standing new job required. The old one was struck and nobody went on strike. The eventual eight rows of steeply stepped timber seating stood the test of not only the few hundreds of that first production but ten years of productions with audiences of up to 120 at a time.

For the first year we laid, on the stepped structure, the borrowed builder's scaffold boards, to provide the actual seating. Then, from 'the takings' of the following year we bought new boards and completed the permanent nature of the seating: seating, mark you with no backs to it (except the be-rugged lower legs of the friendly row above); seating which would have suited the old army usher with the barrack-square voice who crammed 'em in to The Gods of the old Old Vic Theatre with his hoarse 'I want fawty on 'ere!' The human body is as compressible as the occasion is convivial. Ours was an audience of convivial souls. As for the horror you may have at the idea of backless seats: we reckoned that if we couldn't keep our customer's concern rivetted forward on what was happening down on the playing pitch we'd no right to be in the business at all. And it wasn't business, it was love got them there. It *was* business in getting them out. Because, as it had to be, by licence, a private theatre where the public could not pay their way in or be persuaded by advertisement to come, nobody could *buy* a ticket. And, in an Auditorium where every position commanded perfect sight and sound of what was played, we couldn't have put separate prices to seats anyway; an average price for all would have ruined us all and a high price would have meant we were limited to housing the wealthy. So, nobody could buy their way in. They were invited . . . free. But they had to pay their way out!

After the performance – after the audience knew what satisfaction they had in fact been given – two of the players of the play stood at the two exits with two well-loved little baskets in their hands. The exiting audience gave according to its means and according to its satisfaction. This proved to be anything from a 50p piece to a £20 cheque. This was a truer measure of success than any pre-paid ticket for a hoped for satisfaction. It was always a better total than a good average priced ticket would have achieved. And – because much of our economy was based on work freely done and all things imaginatively invented – it *always* covered our production costs.

I said the seating was new boarding – but not bare boards. Another 'growth element' which became permanent was –

THE RED INCREDIBLE CUSHIONS

Again the roving eye of the Auditorium's creator resulted in a phone call:

' . . . In the yard at Norman and Burts' (building experts in church restoration in the City of London but local to the next small township South, Burgess Hill) 'there's a pile in the shed of long horse-hair stuffed pew cushions. Do a treat for the Auditorium. Didn't Norman and Burts do some work for you at Old Place before we did? I did some of my apprenticeship in their shop. Foreman carpenter's name is . . . '

James went along, prepared to use Celtic customer charm. Under a tin roof and trailing out into a puddled yard was the pile of long church pew squabs in faded clerical red; hardly theatrical red plush but indestructable and apparently unwanted. The head of the firm showed willing and passed the matter on to the foreman. 'Well, we're supposed to burn them' (Jesu Maria!) 'But we would be prepared to *buy* them'. And their proposed service to the Arts of Theatre was explained to the foreman. 'Can't do that. But . . . well . . . we could *lend* them to you' . . . pause 'indefinitely'. And for the indefinite future they were imperishably there, labelled row 'A' to 'H' left or right. Having a comfortable, if faded, red they added a glow to the Barn's Auditorium every time the House lights came up, the Music came on and the audience came in. They are still there, stacked under cellophane sheeting along row 'H'; where the one element of, or rather on, John's Auditorium was allowed to lightly rest against the Barn wall – the human back. Any of the audience privileged to get up to that point of vantage first, had a back to the seat: the Barn wall where the owl holes were. Row 'H' was almost level with the height of the great tie beams, from whose level that first flood light, to which the two doves had flown, had flooded the Barn with its first theatrical light.

It is worth stressing again that the Barn was not 'turned into a theatre' and then plays produced in it. It, step by step, grew from the needs of each production. So let's itemize these physical changes brought about in the Barn by the requirements of the first production, and why:

The Auditorium, because simply we now had to *seat* an audience.

The Lighting Booth, with a new connection from the electricity mains and wiring to the booth of some borrowed dimmers and hired lights; because from the start it was obvious that Lighting would be more important than scenic setting, in a playing area inviting free movement and fluent change.

A Prompt Corner, off-stage but within the Barn, because apart from the normal comfort in the presence of an alert prompter, we were plunging in with only two professionals and an untried amateur cast.

A Sound Control, because music and sound effect were built in to the play and a disc or tape deck would need wiring to two splendid gift speakers (high up and masked from the audience's view with more hessian!). This was the nearest to High Tech we ever went. (These speakers were in fact a gift from Andrew Bruce, a young neighbour who became the brilliant source of all the Sound and High Tech effects for *Evita, Cats, Starlight Express,* etc; and whose father and mother regularly helped in productions at the Barn).

As to *Staging or Setting*, apart from the need suitably to screen the old entrance door from the cowsheds (What? Hessian again! Yes, *but* this was no makeshift. Weathered hessian, mellow old oak timbers, elm boards and Sussex clay are all of the one harmony in colour and texture too.) apart from that screening there was the hanging on-stage of an old oak door that squeaked, to cue into a line in the script; also a few more hay bales for 'the stable' and to serve as a platform basis for Herod's throne. That was all that Staging of the play required; no built stage; no – nor ever any 'proper stage' or any boxed-in 'set', which would offend the freedom of this place of free imagination.

We never moved into even the average sophistication of the Technological Age in Lighting, Sound etc. Yet within a sort of simplicity we kept the artistic commitment made in the Dedication, to do our best 'in all the Arts of Theatre; in Sound, Light, Sight and Touch'.

'Touch' is an aesthetic provision that is, as difficult to pin down as it is essential. What is meant here, by Touch, is not that affected fashion (started with the musical *Hair*) of breaking out of the proscenium arch and presuming to render old theatres more intimate by getting down into the auditorium to, physically, touch the (mostly embarrassed) audience. 'Touch' is general and comes from a fully alerted sense of meaningful tangibility as between say, player and players, player and costume, player and props handled, players and scenic elements, and can come right down to the dimming of a light or the fading of a sound with the right sensitivity in the proper rhythm of the play.

Perhaps the point is made by the hessian robe of Joseph (a carpenter). It was painted with a sort of fantasy on the grain patterns of wood; and, during rehearsal, when in a scene of distress over the breaking-strain put on Mary by the birth he moved close to the Barn's old wooden walls, he was alerted to the grain and strength of those enduring timbers, then directed to touch them, feel them and take this carpenter's sense of the worth of wood, and the strain it would stand, into his character and consciousness. Which the actor did and felt from it a new sense of reality come into his lines:

'For I know the woods with which I work
and I know that no wood will stand more strain
than, in the structure of its grain,
it has the natural strength to withstand
But in his desire to create may not God – may not he
overtax the nature of flesh, and she . . . Oh, Mary, Mary! . . . '

Everything tended to be of the Barn, hand-made and manually operated; always tangible. In fact one could almost talk about what went on in the Barn as Tangible Theatre: nothing 'programmed' out of reach or unaccountably and trickily technical. It's not stretching language too far to say that the audiences' surprise at seeming to be 'so in touch' with what was happening in the play had little to do with proximity and a lot to do with being given their freedom easily to identify (through their senses) with what was simply and sense-ably, 'tangibly' happening 'before their eyes'. It was the Theatre of the Imagination – of players *and* audience – rather than the on-stage Theatre of Illusion that the Barn was blessedly stuck with at the start; and retained to its end.

But – not to make these too general claims – let's get back to the practicalities! Firstly, *Lighting* and that 'hutch'. The necessary electrical wiring was done to approved standards by a senior civil servant and MBE, (then working on the computers of Her Majesty's Treasury paying out most of the pensions of Her Majesty's subjects). He too was a total stranger to Theatre, other than to a tip-up plush seat, sort of theatre; most of whose products he uncritically and generously enjoyed.

Small of stature but hugely dynamic, Ray Heavens was appropriately named, being God's gift of light to us; whatever his humanely level-headed agnosticism. He had already expertly – and safely – wired the local cricket pavilion and now began to deserve the addition to his MBE of a DSO for active service in the field of theatre; perilously wiring and fixing lights up in the Barn's high beams. And fixing anything into iron-hard vintage oak beams is no white-collar assignment. Getting the gift of a heavy old spotlight up our longest haystack ladder, to fix in a position between the queen posts (where it would be the light of the Star above Bethlehem) this was more of a spiderman's assignment.

A quick thinker of Napoleonic stature and mental grasp, neighbour Ray came attracted out of a mixture of curiosity and social concern. On arrival he had said, 'Oh? . . . Nativity Play . . . Not my cup of tea really, religious plays. *Emmanuel* – no – never heard of it.' For the moment he had sat and watched some rehearsal. Several years later he wondered what coincidence was. When re-framing a picture for his son there dropped out of its backing a faded, carefully folded page of an old Radio Times. This announced the BBC production of a Christmas play called *Emmanuel* by James Forsyth!

At this moment he was just a curious, if not sceptical watcher. But, seeing the play being made subject to the arts of Theatre – especially the first effects of the art of Lighting – he murmured, 'It *does* grow on you, doesn't it?' Then – the revelation came for Ray – 'I can see that wrong lighting could *ruin* the whole play, Well, couldn't it?' Our neighbour was hooked. And from then on he wired and he operated our lighting for all the years until he had a heart-attack (not utterly unrelated to the addition of the technical tension of a Barn First Night to too much overwork for the Treasury). He had then to settle for continuing only as Honorary Treasurer to the Barn Theatre.

About the Booth. There was no hope of building a solid booth within the limited accommodation of the Auditorium, where at the back it would have commanded a full view of the whole playing area. John, the carpenter and his gang improvised instead a sort of high-level hutch to the west side of the seating and up under the slope of the old stone slab roof. It was screened off from the audience by – yes, hessian; but with a fair view forward of the Deck, or threshing floor and most of the far Slope.

For the lighting operator, Ray, hunched up in this hutch with little heat from anything except three hired wall dimmers – and with draughty gaps in the Horsham stone roof not far from his left ear – it must in that winter have been like squatting within a sort of high level medieval fridge.

Yet – with various measures to discourage the draughts in the chill of winter and encourage them in the heat of summer (and a constant hope that any volunteers for assistant lighting operator would be something below 5 foot 5) we never altered the position of the lighting booth, just solidly partitioned it off and improved its masking and view. The same short ladder to get you up there still stands there today.

However, in its second year a most significant piece of lighting equipment arrived. It well serves now to illustrate the idea of Tangible Theatre. This was a redundant lighting console, gift from a colleague of James in the early Old Vic days, the stage carpenter at The Vic and professional back-stage technician, John Terry; known in the profession as 'Swifty' (because of the speed both of his thinking and his action). Lean and tough as an able seaman under sail, and with the profile of a Paris aristo, he spoke with a Cockney speech and with the greatest intelligence on anything to do with historic London and historic Theatre. John became, for love of it, unsung, unpaid, Technical Advisor to The Barn. He also bequeathed to us, at no cost but the collecting of it, a whole load of stuff when he had to move a life-time's theatrical stores from storage in a redundant station at Bexhill-on-Sea. One item we got into the self-drive van was this 5 foot high by 3 by 4 foot lighting console which looked, in the design of its iron solidity, as if we'd brought away with us a part of the steam age of the station.

A special staging was built from the sandstone up, to take the weight of the console and set it level with our high 'hutch'. When the two Barn Johns – former stage carpenter and present master carpenter – had got it into position in the extended Lighting Booth, the whole hutch looked like a small version of a Steam Age signal box. The console had six dimmers enclosed in its metal casing which were operated manually by smooth worn wooden handles sticking up through channelled slots in its curved casing; like beer pulls in a pub. These were pulled or pushed in a smooth arc (once we'd rid it of rust) from 1 to 10 – fade up, fade down.

And, to fade up or dim down, while gripping these vintage handles and watching the on-stage action away down there on the playing area, this was Tangible Theatre all right, for it was to feel, from head to heart right down through muscle of shoulder arms and fingers, an in-action part of the play as it played, minute by minute, second by second. All off-stage technicians should be respected as if they are a sort of off-stage players, active in their relation to the performance. For instance, an ideal stage-crew (as in the days of sail they may have been) would be a ship's crew accustomed to standing by, on watch and 'knowing the ropes' when action was asked for. Just as an audience, by its evoked imagination can fully 'play their part' with and to the play, everyone in the theatre event can, at best, be participant. One is reminded of Tyrone Guthrie's direction to the young student ushers for the Stratford Ontario Festival Theatre, rehearsing the drill of showing the audience to their seats, 'You are the players before the play.'

Not only an actor prepares; ideally. But the point is made; there was, in the Barn, nothing automatic, pre-programmed, pre-arranged, but always of the minute; renewed as if – like the dialogue of the players as they spoke – it was happening for the very first time. After all, the lighting operator, having the creative freedom to alter by muscle-touch the fading of his lights minute by minute as it was required for the action *actually happening* on-stage – this was simply underlining the nature and constant novelty of *Live* Theatre; where no minute of a play being played is ever the same, let alone any performance of the whole play; nor is the reaction of the audience ever the same as audiences before.

Enough of the immediacy and the tangibility of true theatre, but our non-technological, manual and tangible bias was the Theatre's sort of Back to Nature: the nature being human nature and the communication of this very communal art being as direct as possible.

I think that for this enthusiastic theoretical outburst I have to apologise for breaking the promise to keep observations in the third person. I *did* say that the implications for the Arts and others might be more important than what we did in fact do. Back to the practical evolution.

Prompt and Sound Control were both accommodated in the one off-stage area and nestled beneath the same huge slope of the Barn's west roof; they were on ground level – unlike the lighting hutch – and within the partitioned off bay immediately to the west of the Slope. For a time the tudor brick floor of this highly useful immediate off-stage sort of lean-to gave off a sinister faint smell of 20th Century insecticide or weed-killer; until the days of the former farmer's use of it, to store his drums of such had faded into the distance. *Prompt* had a desk, stool and small electric heater, established in the angle of slotted antique oak boarding of the wall of the booth which most projected on to the edge of the playing area. An actor DSR on the Threshing Floor's deck could swing his ear within a foot of her – as the Prompt scanned text in action under a hooded light. Very handy the gaps in the old boards for scanning the playing area; and the audience.

In this same ground level bay under the lower slope of the stone roof the *Sound Control* table was set; with a good sidelong view through one of the doorway entries we made through the oakboard partitioning on to the playing area. In fact not only did this side bay provide two up-stage right entrances but through its back wall we made a little sneak doorway leading to and from the backstage area of the cowsheds. Other than these facilities it provided an observation spot where the producer or stage manager could sneak in and take a good calm look at the state of the production on-stage with a better than most 'in the wings' view of the action.

Apart from this intimately close off-stage area, all backstage requirements were accommodated in the two long cowsheds attached to the North End of the Barn.

THE COWSHED DRESSING ROOM

For this first production all that was done in the cowsheds was to involve several week-end willing hands, under the active and amiable direction of Louise, in completing what she herself had begun, of uncaking dry cow-dung and doing a great deal of whitewashing of walls; with the same treatment to the curved concrete walling between each couple of cow mangers. We had realised that this farthest east cowshed could make a marvellous communal dressing-room for the players if we fitted some sort of table tops over the floor level mangers and their dividing walls. This was done by a retired ship's architect, a resident at the village end of the lane. A variety of gift mirrors flooded in and Ray's gang wired each dressing table for lights.

After the heavy gang had concreted in the open runnel which ran along the vintage quality floor within backside range of the twitchy tails of the former four-legged, lady occupants, this – the east cowshed – became a Dressing Room that had more space, more light, more happiness – and much better views of the world outside – than any West End or Broadway equivalent; and certainly more immediate and lively relation to the action (one clear cowshed away) in 'the theatre'.

A plasterboard ceiling nailed up to the cross beams, designed to stop the heat escaping through the peg-tiled roof, and two washbasins introduced to the far east end (with a second-hand Sadia for hot water), and we had finished this friendly place where a family atmosphere prevailed. There was no need for sexual segregation here where that coveted status symbol 'Number 1 Dressing Room' was one half of a shared cowstall.

And, if some of this sounds like a rustic and amateur giggle, don't forget that nothing was done 'for the fun of it' and those who came thinking so, soon left and never knew the joy of the end product as it was shared with those who came, not for entertainment but 'nourishment'.

The adjacent cowshed – going towards the Barn – we came to call *The Prom* because we kept it more or less clear except for a Props cupboard and table and also a *Stage Management* table. These were both by the stage entrances, to control and check the players going on or coming off stage and carrying their personal props. But, towards the Dressing Room end of this remarkably spacious backstage area which

THE FORSYTHS' BARN THEATRE
JUBILEE PLAY FOR 1977

"ADELAISE"

22nd

Below: The shore scene in *Adelaise*. The auditorium, showing the gibbet beam and brace *(The Other Heart)*, and one of the owl holes.

Right: Geoffrey Robertson as Albini, Colin Fry, and Peter Searl as Henry I in *Adelaise*.

Left: Edward Lawrence as the Fool Stuff in *Adelaise*.

Right: James Forsyth as Old William in *The Other Heart*.

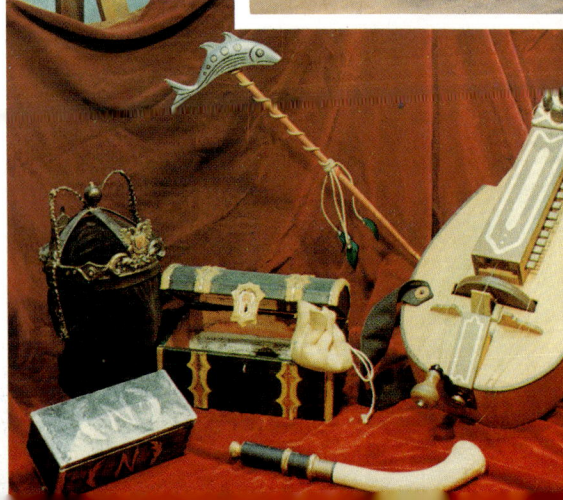

Above: A display of costumes in the Barn.

Right: Geoffrey Robertson as Private Purviance in *Lobsterback!*

Below: A display of properties.

THE FORSYTHS' BARN THEATRE
Ansty -- Sussex

SUMMER 1975 PRODUCTION

"LOBSTERBACK!"

FRIDAY 20th JUNE at 8 pm.
SATURDAY 21st JUNE at 1 pm. and 7.30 pm.
SUNDAY 22nd JUNE at 1 pm. and 7.30 pm.
****

THE FORSYTHS' 1
SUMMER PROI
~ 197!

7th, 18th, 19th, 20th, 21st, 22nd, 23rd.

PROGRAMME

Above: A scene from *N for Napoleone.*

Right: A scene from *A Time of Harvest.*

RODUCTION   THE
O.   Ans

"WENCESLAS"

PERFORMANCES:

February 14th, 15th, 16th and 17th
1980

Please NO SMOKING

Above: The dance of Ruth (Noraini Ariffin) in *A Time of Harvest.*

Left: The whipping post, *The Other Heart.*

![James and Louise]

James and Louise.

The Barn before the auditorium – standing room only!

Above: The Maypole on the Barn Green.

Below: The cowshed as dressing-room.

Louise in the cleaned-o East cowshed.

Left: Paul Gregory, David Knight and Tom Criddle.

Right: Peter Willison, Jack Rothstein and Howard Blake.

came to be carpeted (both for comfort and for SILENCE during performance too) there was a buffet counter; at least that's what it looked like when covered with a long clean table cloth. And in the interval audiences would crowd in to promenade under cover, chat and receive their cups of coffee or tea and biscuits. In fact under its cloth it had a top two inches deep in solid wood with all the stability needed for all the choppery of Butchery. It had been used for many years to demonstrate the cuts of beef to 'young ladies of quality' not a few of whom would be ambassador's daughters. Like most things in the Barn Theatre it came from local resources, in this case from the gracious lady who from her name you would expect to run a taut ship – Frieda Fairbrace. A friend of the Forsyths, she was at this time ceasing to be the owner of the great manor of Cuckfield Park, where for years she had run with commanding skill a residential college of domestic science. Giving up the great house in that year of the advent of the Barn Theatre, she had given us several well-worn carpets of quality not normally met with in a cowshed, about twenty stout chairs, the great kitchen table which the costume ladies found invaluable for cutting-out and this monumental 'buffet', invaluable in the intervals.

During performance players preparing to go 'on-stage' could be seen slowly stalking the carpeted SILENCE of The Prom, as though Stanislavski's ghost trod at their heels, working themselves into their parts in the play.

At the western end, beyond the Props table and opposite the sneak entrance into the off-stage west bay, was a small farm office which had become a storehouse for the Sound equipment and also a Quick-Change Room. Beyond that was the door leading to the outside to the west yards; a door whose location in other theatre buildings would make it the Stage Door.

From all of this perhaps it is obvious how the great Barn with its side bays and its attached long low building of two end-to-end solid cow-byres, so naturally accommodated Auditorium, Playing Area, Light and Sound Booths and all the Backstage requirements of a basic Theatre. And add to the backstage area the south barnyard; where, in the Summer sun, audiences could spill out from the Prom during the interval; or where the company could recline in deckchairs or spread themselves on the dry grass during breaks in rehearsal.

But we get ahead of the developments.

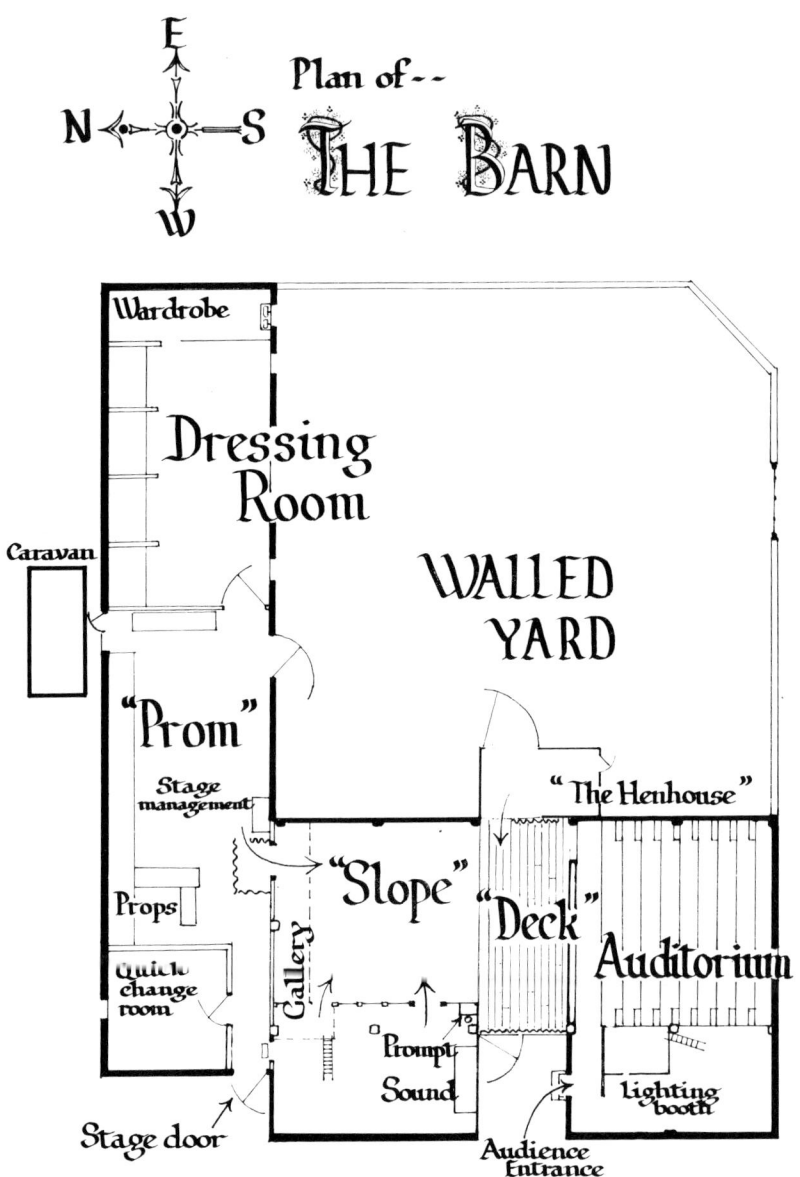

Plan of--
THE BARN

N E S W (compass)

Wardrobe

Dressing Room

Caravan

WALLED YARD

"Prom"

Stage management

"The Henhouse"

Props

"Slope"

"Deck"

Gallery

Auditorium

Quick change room

Prompt

Sound

lighting booth

Stage door

Audience Entrance

CHAPTER FOUR

If crisis No. 1 for us was the question of a Licence (not for liquor but for a 'playwright's workshop theatre, limited to an invited audience and 21 days of performance in any one year') then crisis No. 2 was any theatre's twentieth century headache – *Parking*. Because, beyond the first production we had to look to the day when the quality of Sussex field mud or the non-availability of an agriculturally precious farmer's field might well defeat us. Crisis No. 3 was temperamental and internal and had to do with the difficult mix of players between professional and amateur. But of that later.

PARKING

For the reasonable sort of rustic event of a nativity play in an old Barn the friendly farmer was willing to supply a fair area of the nearest field. Years later one could have seen the alarming sight of a great combine harvester stuck, up to its axles, in the same field, but at this time our farmer was almost as new to the fields as most of us were to running a theatre (with the exception of he who played Herod, from his throne on a dais of bales of straw – Henry Sherwood, a West End theatre impresario). The farm manager's stalwart son, Paul Fisher, who was later to be a startlingly original Tony Lumpkin, stood by with a tractor, in case any car should get badly bogged down.

The First Night for *Emmanuel* came, on a December afternoon. On the 'Order of the Day' on James's clipboard, at the place where it read '2 pm Company Call ... Bill Garforth check field and parking signs ...' the tractor was there, ticking over comfortably in the wan light of what had been a wet day, with an authoritative Major Bill Garforth standing by several bales of generously donated dry straw.

We got all cars off the puddly lane and into the field under our one-legged Major's direction and, as the normal sort of parking-lot salvo of slamming doors died away, the audience had all walked – as that first ever audience had done, partly on a path of straw – towards the glow of light beginning to show from the Barn; and in they went with not too much apprehension of being able to get away again when they came out. When they did there was the further comfort, under the night sky, of tractor's headlights illuminating the field.

As it was certainly not just the quality of the accruing equipment of the Barn Theatre but the quality of the growing number of supporters which gave it punch and appeal, a word should be said about Major Bill

Garforth and his command of the car park. In our complete social mix he was our second ex-regular Army representative. The first had been ex-CSM Clifford Smith, formerly of the Coldstream Guards and presently i/c of the Ansty cross-roads village store. He, for this first production, had been promoted from shoveller-out of dry cattle dung to 'Front of House Manager', controlling Auditorium, rugs for audience knees etc.

Bill Garforth and his wife Rosemary – both I would say deeply possessed, through service and distinguished family record, of the better graces of the British Raj and our great Imperial Past – were among the first and most loyal volunteers at the Barn. Rosemary took charge of Props and was a rather beautiful and constant presence backstage by the Props cupboard and table, seeing players going on and off stage. Bill was o/c Parking, for which he adopted as uniform the fluorescent orange type of plastic jerkin worn by rail workmen on the nearby London/Brighton line. He was also our first Dan-Dan the Sanitary Man; o/c Loos redolent of Field Training conditions. He had lost one leg in the War, but never lost courage anywhere. Full o' fun, he was as commandingly firm as he was courteous. To in-coming drivers of all social rank, up to circuit judge, 'Do as I say,' never had to be said. He sounded and looked like authority; even off duty with piss-full pails in his hands. He, or the farmer, or someone, had heard somebody say – who had been part of the Chipperfield Circus crew – 'Give me straw! – give me straw and I'll get any vehicle away out of a field.'

After the play – even in the dark of the evening performance with the matinee cars having somewhat ploughed up its surface before – the tractor, its headlights throwing the strawy ruts into high relief, did all necessary recovery. And with shouts, pushes, busy torches shining and storm lanterns swinging, all cars were got out of the field and away up the muddy lane. One ardent young parking assistant pushing at the rear of a roaring car came back into the light of the now empty Barn spattered from face to shin with as many mud-spots as a collander has holes.

But for these three audiences for three performances the evidence of reaction, beyond the immediate applause, began to come back in, and to prove that their mini-pilgrimage to the Barn and this bit of drama had been a bit more than worthwhile. 'Do more' would again be the common request. And – worth noting now – this sense of mini-pilgrimage to an improbable temple of Drama was part of the value of the event.

'One of the most fascinating and theatrically exciting experiences of recent years . . . '

Brighton and Hove Gazette

'Mud and general dampness failed to diminish the occasion thanks to the lines of Mr Forsyth, a fluent and imaginative production ... and a large company that included some well-known professionals, and the sheer perfection of the setting for the work.*

'Although it glows with vision and throughout has a poetic ring, there is nothing Christmas-carol about *Emmanuel*. Its naturalism reflects the realistic social side of Mr Forsyth's work, but, whether in darkness or flooded with Rembrandtesque light, the hero of the night was the Barn itself.

Mid Sussex Times

This brings up again the question, recently echoed by a former worker in the Barn. 'What *was* it, which hooked us all – and made it all so effective; and affecting?'

'Was it the Barn itself? – or – I don't know. Difficult to pin down.' And it is, but perhaps to take his nostalgic comments, and those of another quite different worker at the Barn, and look at them at this point may serve the main purpose of the book; which is to pursue the implications of our small-scale success for the help this might be for larger, fully 'professional' theatres.

Remember that all players and production team came from an area within one hour's travelling-time from the Barn, and most of our audience resided in those five small townships and villages, Ansty, Cuckfield, Haywards Heath, Bolney and Burgess Hill; which gave it a neighbourly comradeship to all involved, unlike large town Theatre.

Peter Coveney of Burgess Hill, was an electronics engineer whose theatrical talents till this time had been used by his local Theatre Club to run their sophisticated Sound system. Burgess Hill has the character of a small boom town in light industry. His wife, a highly intelligent and robust teacher in a junior school, was about the most efficient amateur stage-manager around, whose services James grabbed when free. Peter was built to a small and fine scale of Creator's blueprint and committed to a day to day form of heroism in by-passing crippling rheumatoid arthritis to get on with the work. He had a neat beard, a saint's smile and when he eventually did duty in our Sound Booth the stage carpenters had to find an extra step to get his chin the right height

---

*In a later year when the Vicar of the local church asked James to bring the production of *Emmanuel* to the Church in Cuckfield, he said he was flattered but, 'No. It is most at home in the Barn. In the Church it would become a Religious Drama play. It is a folk play – deeply religious in nature. Sorry.' Then he was more flattered still when the Vicar brought his whole family service congregation across the valley and to a performance in the Barn. The professionals included David Knight and the humorist Basil Boothroyd.

above the tape deck. Two immensely strong characters, Margaret and he, and no strangers to hard work.

Earlier that year Peter was brought in to advise on the techniques and safety precautions to be faced in fixing up wiring and amplifying our two gift loud speakers. He had therefore seen and known the Barn in its original state but until this first *Emmanuel* he had not seen it in use. So, what was his first impression of it as a theatre.

'Well – extraordinary – but difficult to define. When Margaret and I were seated up there' (and not the most comforting seating for someone in constant pain from knees and hips) 'watching the play I experienced something I just had never experienced before in all my experience of Theatre. I just don't know; it was the whole atmosphere . . . it glowed . . . the appearance, the action . . . Yes, it had to do with the play, the playing, the production . . . the whole thing . . . whole atmosphere . . . difficult to pin down, but I know we were hooked.'

Of course it was the Barn itself 'the hero of the night' affecting him, but this sense of the 'whole thing' could be the all-arts terms of the Dedication-to-come already at work. 'And may it always be the best we can do in *all* the Arts of Theatre; in Sound, Light, Sight and Touch.'

Dick Walker was another early volunteer worker. A jovial broad shouldered, broad-faced, broad-fingered, redhead with bleached eye-lashes, bleach blue eyes and a smile always just ahead of his sportsman's readiness, steadiness and go. Son of a wealthy city merchant he established a notable family in Cuckfield – notably large in these times – of three sons and three daughters, and established thereafter three or four successful sports shops in the neighbouring towns.*

Dick, when questioned recently: 'What drew you to the Barn in the first place?' answered,

'Oh, I'd heard James read, several years before, some of his poems in a musical evening in a neighbour's house and admired the man. So when I heard of this venture in the Forsyths' Barn, I got myself and my wife Margaret invited along.'
'And liked what you saw?'
'Quite frankly, I was overwhelmed by what we saw. And I felt impelled to write to him and Louise, offering to help in any way I could; thought it was a marvellous idea. I remember the earthen stage, the ancient rough timbers of the walls, all so in the spirit and the colour of the original

---

*Recently an innocent victim of a near-fatal road accident, in which he broke most of his limbs and lost his sight, his indomitable spirit has got him back to work in a remarkably full life. In the quality of the people that the barn seemed to attract we were blessed with all kinds of courage.

Nativity story. And the cast were really outstanding with an impression of utter simplicity and devotion to what they were saying and doing.'

'One thing I remember saying in my letter was that they could be sure of drawing an enthusiastic audience from the immediate locality and that it could be the beginning of something that could grow and grow.'

Three things perhaps became apparent now about the basis for success. 1. This wholeness of the artistic effort, in service to the play. (A question of theatre arts). 2. The acceptance of 'the atmosphere' of the Barn itself and the production presented within and never in conflict with its visual quality. (A question of architecture and design). 3. The hospitable totality of the event; within which the event of the play took place. (A question of celebration, of occasion and care for people; Louise's sphere).

This latter was peculiarly important to the Barn Theatre and can stand stressing again. It was partly *because* it was an achievement to get there, and that it was a unique place when you did get there, that gave the audience the feeling of a special event in a special place. Very unlike going to either the village hall or one of a number of theatres off a city street. (The classic example of special theatre, special place is the Greek Delphi or Epidaurus.)

And on hospitality – the welcoming atmosphere of an event. This was an audience of neighbours, friends and friends' friends. And that's how the future Barn audiences grew by friendly report, not by advertisement and publicity or people buying tickets, but by wanting to go, asking how and being invited. James would always proudly say, 'Nobody can buy their way into my theatre.' But anybody who asked would be invited. And when, later on we formed our supportive association of Friends of the Barn, and somebody new would say, 'Can I pay my subscription?', Louise would say, 'No. You'll be invited and if you like your first Barn event and it likes you, then you can give an annual £2 donation.' (To be used for our maintenance needs of the following year.) As Dick Walker said:

'In fact Louise was the personification of the Barn's hospitality. People came to expect and to love to find her standing there by the Programme Sellers at the little audience entry door, clipboard in hand and welcoming all who, from being names on her meticulous Card Index came to be the familiar faces of a sort of extended family and for whom she greatly cared. A small woman, shy in fact of strangers but strong in warmth and will: goodwill.

'I suppose the basis of the sense of welcome and hospitality was that it was their homestead where it all happened and they between them took an overall and personal responsibility for the total event. Hence the clipboard carried by each and the sense, to an unusual degree that everything, and everybody, related'

Again we come back to the whole 'atmosphere' of not just the Barn but what was 'in the air'. Some of the old 18th Century and older town theatres had all this sense in their structure and decor which creates a sense of embracing one in an atmosphere of welcoming anticipation. Some of the new amphitheatre playhouses also create this sense of special anticipation of what is going to take place on their open stage. And this no blank screen, TV or Film can have. 'Going to the Theatre' has always been the antithesis of 'switching on the TV', or even 'going to a film'. In an age of Convenience, TV has the edge (disreputably) on a self-pampering public. Going to the Barn, by resilient members of our Consumer Goods Society was not just an expedition to savour the wares, or to see an advertised play. The play may have been 'the thing'. But we had not the feeling of 'putting on' or 'presenting' a play. It was never a commodity: to be bought, applauded or approved. It was the central event within the event of 'going to the Barn'. And this was a long way from going to Shaftesbury Avenue to buy one's way in to see a play some critic or crony had told you was worth seeing. And I think the contrast (not to mention the small cost in cash) appealed and made it special.

A special feature of the event took place with no sense of planning – just a sense of care – with the first full production. And again it just happened; then became a persisting convention of Barn events.

This is what we called

THE WELCOME SPEECH

Talking about total atmosphere Dick Walker touched on it when he said . . .

'When we were sitting up there under the great crossbeams in the auditorium, the audience were in and settled down, *and everything went quiet*; then one could feel this total atmosphere; a sort of presence . . . '

What happened in fact was this (all set down on the clipboard and timed to the minute).

1. At the small audience-entry door James checked that the audience was in and gave the 'Stand-ready!' to the Lighting Booth, immediately inside and above his head, then closed the audience entry door and nipped out round and back in through the Stage Door.
2. Warned the Sound Booth and came 'on-stage' and as he came forward Sound faded out the final piece of Music for the assembly of the audience (always designed to lead in to the mood of the play) and Lights faded the Pre-set lighting leaving one spot to isolate him; then
3. He made – for at most 2 minutes – what came to be known as The Welcome Speech. With this the atmosphere of personal care and

humour broke the seriousness, with his standard reminder to newcomers that 'in this theatre you get in free; but you pay to get out'. Two players from the play they had seen would be at the exits with 'the hat'. A word about no smoking, about refreshments in the interval back-stage in the prom; any reference to the hand-painted programmes and then

4. How the playing of a play was a live process the final part of which was its communication to 'you the audience, who are essential to us the players and the production team. It is for, and with you, that we play. Thank you for coming because, really, without you there would be no play. Now to the play.'

And the fade of the house lights would take the audience into the dark as James retired backstage and the play began. The process never changed and the audience who, outside, had been welcomed in by Louise went forward with the play welcomed into it by James, feeling cared for, wanted, and needed.

Granted he had given his reaction to the first production as one of the audience, how had Dick felt as *one of the Company*: because his offer to help in any way had been taken up later in the year when James said he wanted him to play a part in the Summer Production.

'Startled. I'd been content to be helpful in minor ways when the celebration of Christmas was followed by a celebration of Spring (their second event) when the Barn lot invented a be-ribboned, crowned, maypole and children of the neighbourhood in white with floral chaplets were drilled to dance around it to a genuine Sussex fiddler on the Barn Green; prelude to a programme of Music and Poetry celebrating Spring which was given in the Barn. This was the first of a perennial event, *Music in May*.

'With my love of music I shared the almost childlike excitement I saw in James at having fine music shiver the timbers of the old building. It was noticeable too how the first-rate professional musicians then playing a Schubert Trio especially enjoyed playing in the Barn to this sort of neighbourly audience; in contrast to recording studio or large concert hall performance. Howard Blake – our gifted local composer who lived down at the Mill – had got together the violinist, and leader at that time of the London Mozart players, Jack Rothstein, and the distinguished cellist Peter Willison. They agreed with him that in the Barn there was a great sense of not just "performing a piece" but of "making music" almost as, in the old days of original chamber music, musicians *made music* in the great houses to an audience of patrons, friends and neighbours. Again this sense of on-the-spot *making*, creating.

'When he asked me to play a part in a play! Well – I'd done next to no acting. But this was before I knew that James did not like the acting of actors. He liked the playing of players. I suppose there is a sort of self-centred flavour of exhibitionism about Acting. And anybody exhibitionist enough to put themself above service to the play and its service to the audience wasn't encouraged to parade their talent at the Barn.'

'A bit of a tyrant?'

'Well – the discipline was tough. He was a hard taskmaster if you like, and drove himself hard to get through a lot of work in not a lot of rehearsal time. It was Louise, with her protective care for the others involved, who would often call a halt to rehearsal and call him a slavedriver. But we weren't slaves. We knew what was driving him. It was there in the Dedication; something we wanted to strive for too; and at the best level of excellence we were capable of. And my capability was pretty low level. But he seemed to me to have a special genius for commanding the loyalty and service of a group of people having total diversity of occupation, age, upbringing, outlook etc; and of welding together, by a common devotion to an artistic end, a collection of quite different levels of talent and skill.'

'You, Dick, have said a lot – and in obvious personal admiration of the Artistic Director; what about the Administrative Director, Louise?'

'Genius in her field too. Hyper-efficiency is the label I, as a business man, attach to my memories of Louise: efficient, but nothing ever cold about Louise; as firm in will as she was soft at heart: a little lady constantly on the move shuttling to and fro between her secretarial set-up in the house ("Grainloft" at this time) and the backstage departments of the Barn, attending to questions of Costume, Tickets, Programme content, Telephone; with only occasional surreptitious visits to James' field of operations in the theatre: not uncommonly concluded by her clear voice suddenly calling out from up by the owl hole on Row "H", "Can't *hear!* – must hear." She was always practical.'

'Her background wasn't the Arts, was it?'

'No. She created some stunning costumes to James' design but the Social Services and Accountancy were her field. And, from being a student at the London School of Economics to being the incorruptible "Pani-directress" of all the camps for Displaced Persons in the Munich area, after the War, her sphere was the field of Care. In current phraseology, "a very caring person". Someone we could all easily approach and utterly rely upon.

'Not that James was unreliable but sometimes formidable; requiring courage to be approached. But before leaving off on him – having said rather a lot – one unshakeable insistence of his seemed to be greatly to control the down-to-earth but rich quality of the productions. It goes back to my surprise at the *quality* of that first *Emmanuel*, of the colour of the "earthen stage", the golden straw, the warm, worn old timbers, the painted hessian basic to all the costumes. This was his stubborn insistence that all the design and material of costumes, props, setting be originated there and be in what I'd call "the natural product" – natural to the Barn – not ever glossy and never bought, hired or brought in. If one could find the material for the making of a thing already there and native to the Barn, the buildings or countryside, then that was it. When he and John Lower with the set-construction gang made two stagings, but not "a stage", each of these stagings was carpentered to a design James drew and was made from old oak on site and boarding "weathered" by the stage crew to blend with the wooden walls of the Barn.

'In their use for different levels of the action they looked part of the structure that had always been there; similarly with the players and musicians' gallery built later at the up-stage end. It was for *Fifteen Strings of Money*, the first Summer Play, that I played the part of provincial governor Chu-Chen, and during rehearsals I saw how, out in the yard James and his design assistants, in pursuit of "the natural product" had dyed raw linen and hung it to dry along the old post-and-rail fences in the sun; before painting the now coloured natural linen ("natural product") with motives of Chinese folk-art design: lovely costume material for the characters in the play.

'I can also see him using the natural bamboo from Howard Blake's millpond to fashion a backpack for Hsiung Yu-Lan, the chinese packman. The artist in him was happy as a sandboy on that sort of job. By being both designer and director he managed (as one heard Peter Potter,* his friend and colleague, say) to have an unusual integrity of design which ran through most productions. It was in this first Summer production, as I said, that not only the Barn's moveable stagings with their distinctive cornerposts made their debut, but I did as actor; sorry! – player.'

Yes – and it was with this production the Barn directorate of two, and their Policy Group, had to face a crisis to do with human temperament.

CRISIS NUMBER THREE

The play had a large cast (now one of the available luxuries that only the amateur theatre and the subsidised theatre can afford). Of the 25 players required five were professionals (David Knight, Paul Seed, Mavis Taylor-Blake, Jerry Walls and James), though one of those was an "amateur" in this country; Jerry Walls came from Canada whose TV was paid-professional before its Theatre was. His experience was therefore of the category of a professional repertory company player in this country. Jerry, management consultant, and neighbour from the mill cottages, played the principal part in the play (a part which star actors of the classical Chinese Theatre had always grabbed). He played the part by merit of talent, skill and suitability. There was no feeling on the part of our full professionals about this. But ... let me go straight to a note in the minutes of a general meeting held after the production, whose purpose was to consider the future of the Barn Theatre, now that the clamour for it to continue so positively gave it one. I note, from Louise's records, that Liza Hagon, the young actress from the Stratford, Ontario, Shakespeare Festival Theatre, who had found herself in that first New Year's Masque, playing Daughter of

*Peter Potter: TV and Covent Garden producer/director.

Day and Night, was present along with her husband, the actor Garrick Hagon.

Anyway it was a meeting of 38 enthusiasts, and in the old house, in autumn.

The items on the Agenda were four:

1. 'Whether a Club should be formed, with a membership fee.' This didn't have much future, with both the Artistic and Administrative Directors being very anti Clubism and Club Committees; and fees raising little money and lots of moral obligation.
2. 'Whether there should be a charge for tickets or if the policy of free admission with a collection should continue.' Continue it did. Fixing a price was full of problems.
3. 'What kind of approach should be made to various authorities for support.'
   'James said that there had already been the suggestion of help from the Southern Arts Association towards the cost of a lighting board and some adequate heating.'

It is of general interest to note here that after some good but minor help in the hiring of lights and dimmers, the Southern Arts Association went to considerable trouble and agonising about how to help; and finished up by giving one grant of £50 with the request that in all our programmes we state the fact that we were subsidised by the Southern Arts Association. We thanked them, published the fact in one programme that they had given us £50 and went ahead on our own. Their trouble was that they could not or would not give us real support unless we publicized more and made our theatre available to 'the public' and also were prepared to take in other 'shows' and 'companies'. One can understand that their brief was to serve the public in general but our licence was limited to an invited audience, no 'publicity' and 21 days of performance in the year. What we wanted was help to finance the quality we had achieved for service to the already adequate audience we had; not just expand; and lose our unique character. So much for an inflexibility in official patronage of the Arts. But about our internal crisis.

4. 'The question of the mixture of professional/amateur – should this continue or not?'
   'Bill Garforth said that if a Club were formed, local people could not join if it meant that mainly professional players were to be used . . . '
   'Louise pointed out that a large number of people were involved in preparing for, in the rehearsals for, and on the actual performance days. These were all unpaid amateurs who had a limited amount of time to give to the project and were already giving a maximum amount of time.'
   'David Knight – "the professional actor" – spoke on the question of the use of professional players, and the difficulties of trying to combine

amateurs with professionals in the same play. While lovely things had happened in the past productions . . . '

And he described to many of us how he had been startled into new realisations about acting by some of the amateurs, but we also saw how much instruction he had given by the way to grateful beginners who had valued this rubbing of the shoulders with some seasoned professionals. But, he said,

'there were difficulties and in his opinion it would be better to keep it as an amateur community theatre. Professionals have in general not enough time to give the amount of rehearsals needed by amateur players "though there were advantages for both to work together".

'Garrick Hagon brought up the question of a theatre workshop for professionals providing new opportunities for professionals who were hampered by not being able to rent suitable workshop premises etc.'

'Mavis Taylor-Blake suggested that plays could be done with local professionals only with rehearsals of two full weeks and with some tie-up with repertory.'

You can see the separate hopes and ambitions astir. Here is something that will always happen with a new venture at the first signs of real but limited success. It's not just people 'jumping on the band-waggon' in hopes of changing the tune. In rehearsal off-moments there had evidently been some quite understandable aggravation on the professionals' part at the tyranny of James driving them along with the same drive the amateurs needed. In fact Mavis had been heard to say that as James was so evidently happily at home sitting making props in the sun . . . should not he stick to his Art? Frictions unknown in the Barn till then began.

The heart-cry of Garrick (Hagon) for a professional workshop or lab. theatre was an echo of what was being called for by players in the national companies: a studio theatre – small experimental place – a demand which resulted in The Other Place, at Stratford-on-Avon, The Warehouse in London and the standard provision in the big new theatres of the little attached studio theatre. The pressures were afoot which could break the whole project up. One had to decide.

The big decision was made: to swing totally towards James' concept of 'amateurs' fully 'professed' to the Arts of Theatre in the terms of the Dedication. And, if this was so, to arrange somehow for more professional instruction for his 'amateurs' by experienced theatre people. This some of his colleagues in the profession willingly did and for a nominal fee. There had been no hope of paying professional players in the company; nor could they be expected to give time to the Barn when offered lucrative or important parts on TV or in the West End. Louise and James had been witnesses of how dangerously much service David Knight had so generously given to the Barn in its establishment phase – because he loved it and the concept. But, she felt, it was cruel to him, in that he put himself in danger of neglecting London contacts of his professional career. Fair enough this risk for James. It was his theatre; his plays were being worked out. And I agreed. We had to let our 'professionals' go free.

Mavis, who beautifully played the young Su Hsu-Chien, the female lead in the play was, off-stage, bitter; Howard, her husband, tense (but he had freedom to use the Barn for Music). Paul Seed (now a gifted TV director), who played the young packman, and David, who played the incorruptible Judge Kuang (who saves the two young lovers from fatal miscarriage of justice), both remain, to this day, Friends of the Barn whatever distance they are now from it. And the whole production that Summer took the Barn Theatre into international classical comedy – to the delight of 550 and the satisfaction of its Artistic Director.

It seemed that on the earth and the boards of the Barn it might be possible to 'transport' audiences in imagination, to any location – certainly the bamboo province of Wushi. And, in the following Summer, to another rural setting for classical comedy – the Hardcastles' Hall of *She Stoops to Conquer*: when the great additions to the equipment of the Barn were the 'signal box' lighting console to the lighting booth, and the caravan – attached to the Prom as refreshments kitchen. (A second-hand caravan acquired for £20! by John, the carpenter, and internally stripped and adapted by his construction gang to make an immobilised mobile kitchen; with a wildlife view over the back pond where the waterfowl nested.)

THE BARN ORGANIZATION: OR NON-ORGANIZATION

Out of that 1973 general meeting on 'where do we go from here' there emerged the nearest thing to a committee the Forsyths ever allowed – *The Policy Group* we called it. It was simply a resolute group of workers and players devoted to the Barn and its Dedication, adding up, with Louise and James, to ten, who were called together by the Forsyths before and after any event as advisers and critics of procedure and their authority rested upon their intelligence and integrity and the respect James and Louise had for them and vice versa.

They debated round the old octagonal table in the Forsyths' home (Old Place, and then Grainloft). They were far from being yes-men or yes-women to James and Louise; but all final decisions were made by these two following the debate and it was they who bore final responsibility. Only one 'office bearer' was allowed, the Honorary Treasurer (Ray Heavens) and this was simply because Louise in her wisdom considered it best that the Forsyths should not handle the cash.

The whole thing had cost them money till then but the project was not for making them or anyone any money and their benefit over all its time was a) that the takings defrayed a proportion of the rates, b) the Barn, their property, was kept in fair preservation by this good use, c) James had the benefit of putting to test some of his plays. (Though this latter must be offset by the excessive unpaid professional time he spent on an amount of instruction benefitting everybody).

By its personnel the Policy Group covered the field of Barn Theatre activities: Ray Heavens, (Lights and Finance) John Lower (Carpentry and Construction), David Knight and Jerry Walls (Players) Howard Blake (Music), Dick Walker (Work Parties), Rosemary Garforth (Props), Louise (Costume and Administration), Geoffrey Skelton (Author and Drama Critic of Radio Brighton – plays) and James (General Artistic Direction).

Leo Tolstoy, in his attack on the organized institutions of his time, universities, church government, declared that 'organization is a sin'. Not too unlike Tom Paine saying that all Government is a necessary evil. Perhaps it was because James was writing at that time his play on the last days of Tolstoy for Granada TV, that he was so against committees, rules and regulations and anything which would put an organizational straightjacket on the free discipline of the Dedication. Any attempts, therefore, to regularize the Barn away from what was proving in practice to be its effective eccentric self were fended off.

In the next two years these practical improvements for the audience were achieved: a large section of the lane was re-surfaced (costing little expense, except one hernia and one mild heart attack); a surface treatment of the yard area around the Barn with russet tile rubble and 'scalpings' of grey granite (lovely 'natural product' colour scheme) got parked cars off the field and on to the hard, costing a few hundred pounds; also a partitioning and plumbing of the stable gave LADIES and GENTLEMEN improved and more private 'chemical' loos. On the Arts side the Barn Theatre originated four new works – four 'world premiers': two plays, one small opera and one quartet.

The first of the two plays was for a Christmas event to replace *Emmanuel*, which by general request was in danger of becoming the regular winter production and so limiting our repertoire. This was an adaptation done by James of *The Pickwick Papers* given dramatic shape by concentrating upon the rise, fall and resolution of the famous case of Pickwick versus Bardell. Its setting was notable for the contrast of 'scene' the whole playing area could convincingly evoke, between the cold gloom of the Fleet debtor's Prison and the warm busyness of human traffic of Goswell Street. It had a large cast from a growing company of 35.

The second of the plays brought the Barn Theatre fully into its licensed use as 'playwright's workshop theatre'. This was a play commissioned from James by Tufts University in the Boston area, to be a major contribution of the University to the American Bicentennial Celebrations in Boston during 1976. The Bicentenary celebrated the colonial revolution which began in the Boston area, led to War and to the final declaration of American Independence. James chose to work out the play in the Barn and only after its tryout in the Barn with a Barn company to deliver the final script to Boston. This gave the 1975 Summer production the added excitement for all concerned of originating a new work for the professional theatre; and it gave James for the first time the full advantage of his 'workshop theatre'.

The play's action was set in 'a ropewalk on the Boston quays' – where all a ship's cordage was spun – and 'a barn on the Milton Heights overlooking Boston'; settings as at home in the Barn as the Bethlehem stable had been. The 'natural product' dominating the whole atmosphere of the play was rope: in one case the use of a whole curtain of heavy rope hanging from the big crossbeams.

But not to be in any way dismissive about the Music, yet to concentrate on the Drama, a short note on the Quartet. The Barn had evidently inspired Howard Blake to get down to work in creative rebellion against contemporary affectations of all music since Stockhausen, and in the peace of his studio down in the Mill, to write a neoclassical, and lovely quartet, Schubertian in character and played in the 1974 Music in May with professional delight by Jack Rothstein, violin, Peter Willison, cello, Kenneth Essex, viola, and Howard Blake, piano. To the delight of them both, Howard dedicated it to Louise and James.

His second work originating from the Barn was a one-act comic opera (for commuters!) called The Station, set roughly on Platform 3, Haywards Heath on the Brighton line. Wickedly clever in light satirical vein it sent more laughter up into the roof timbers than the Barn could ever before have known; and was repeated on request four years later. With the stagings joined together to be platform and with the deck of the threshing floor becoming imaginatively the 'fast line', the Barn accommodated another, and contemporary, setting surprisingly well.

With Lobsterback! (the term used by Boston's largely fishing community for the invading redcoats) the Barn setting and 'ropewalk' raised little difficulty. And, with a return to the earth and sandstone floor in one section of the Slope and a specially copied replica of a Boston street lamp swung out from the old brick and timbered walls, we had a remarkably convincing 'alleyway in Boston'. This use of sections of the large playing-area separately set with token but substantial and symbolic units, which were then isolated by lighting, became as much a regular convention of Barn productions as the overt scene-change by stage crew, as they did the change in their hessian uniform tabards under a soft flood of coloured light.

A semi-permanent constructional feature added to the Barn as a requirement of *Lobsterback!* was what we called 'The Henhouse'. This was a cooping-in from the outside of the big doorway entrance at the East end of the threshing floor. It gave players a downstage entrance without either standing in rain outside or being accompanied in by billowing curtain when they made their entrances. It was an approximate 6′×12′ housing of 4″×2″ timbers and weatherboarding, roofed with corrugated iron which we had to cover over with a tough old tarry stagecloth from the Old Vic; a covering not just to render the Henhouse more in period with the Barn's aesthetic but to deaden on a rainy day the staccato rhythm of drops from roof gutter high above.

This large external hutch was a most useful addition to the Barn's theatrical architecture. It gave us a downstage entrance and also let us throw some lighting in from it on to the Deck. Most important of all, it gave us a wide opening to off-stage. To this the audiences' attention could be directed by the action of the play and led on by the on-stage player's words to a whole world of imagination. By this one could create a whole off-stage world of the play not contained within the Barn walls. Its first effective use was by a player in this play describing her love of this Massachusetts barn with its view – which she was then 'looking down towards' – of Boston, with its distant forest of masts of the shipping lying in the harbour.

In the same production, when treating the Deck, of the threshing floor, as the deck of a ship in the Boston harbour, the Henhouse served a spectacular use. That bit of the Bulwark which we had been obliged by fire regulations to cut away (to give free flow of exiting audience from Auditorium to deck exits) was hinged to swing across the exit to the Henhouse and in the action was treated as bulwark to the British man-o-war. Over it our young lobsterback climbed – to 'jump down into the cold sea' – (as the outraged Sergeant tried to harpoon him with his halberd).

The actor playing the young redcoat became a semi-permanent addition at that time to the Barn community. For Geoffrey Robertson was a gifted and highly intelligent player, trained for 'the profession' at LAMDA (the London Academy of Music and Dramatic Art), but who became a teacher at his father's Sussex School within our area.

Another important factor was noted by Peter Searl, an architect who joined us at this time. It was that the whole of the production was – in his terms – 'built, like the old Barn itself had been, *on site*'. He didn't mean just physical construction, but that the concept of the production was visualised by the producer, walking the Barn, thinking it out there, or sitting up in the Auditorium 'dreaming' through the play's action while staring down at the playing area. And that from there on, bit by accumulative bit, the building of concepts of character, costume, props, setting, sound effect, lighting scheme was all created there 'on site' where the final 'building', the performance, would be; with the atmosphere and quality of the Barn breathing through it all; that any player in rehearsal would see the costumes in creation by 'Louise's ladies' who could at any time down scissors and needles on the big kitchen table in the Dressing Room and walk through to the Theatre where they could see the players in play for whom they were making the costumes; that the producer could try out an incomplete prop or costume, in action. And that at Coffee Time in the evenings or weekends, all present, from Admin, Direction, Stage Management, Sound, Lighting and the Stage Crew on set construction* could be together in lively chat; with the Producer checking progress on all fronts as things grew together towards performance; *there*.

Except for some national companies and Civic companies with their own theatres, you really don't get this sort of free and fruitful rubbing of shoulders between all departments of the theatre arts, crafts and admin. Seldom ever can it be fully achieved in the Amateur Theatre, where so often a production has to be brought forward in bits and pieces in different places and, at the last minute (because halls cost lots to hire) brought together into a village hall and on to a stage better suited for the platform party of a local association than for theatrical performance. For any company to have its own theatre at its disposal throughout production is a huge advantage.

Peter Searl, who became one of our principal players, joined the company in a typical way. He came to accompany his youngest son, who was rehearsing in the Pickwick play; saw how the boy was not just being lumped in as an extra but was being taught to pitch his voice so that he could effectively be seen to be selling 'Fresh fish!' in the stage hubbub of Dickens's Gosling Street. The arts of theatre and the family feeling of the company hooked him and the architect he was began to be the actor he naturally was.

Added – for the comfort of the audience – at this time were two large electric fan heaters to either side of the Auditorium. And it was expenditure on such 'capital expenses' as this and the improvements to the parking, hard-standing and the lavatories, that required monies beyond the means of the production budgets or the Forsyths' freelance finances; which were then in a somewhat invalid state.

The Friends of The Barn was therefore brought into being. By paying a yearly donation of £2 per person (over 9 years it was never necessary

---

*A firm principle applied by the Artistic Director was that those who handled the pieces of setting in performance should be those who had built them.

to increase it) a Friend of The Barn was entitled to invitation to all events and any general reports on progress sent out.

One final improvement to the amenities, which the funds of The Friends now provided for, was the new and extensive parking area in the paddock which lay only a few yards walk away to the north of the Barn: the normal grazing area of 'Pax' the surviving sheep.

It was in this year, 1976, that the Forsyths got back into solvency (the life of a freelance artist has waves and troughs) by selling the big house of Old Place to a youngish family and using not quite all the proceeds to convert the little granary to a delightful dwelling for their latter years. By this move they could stay close by the Barn. The temptation had come, been faced and passed by, of doing 'the sensible thing' – selling up the whole property, barn, land and all and going, richly endowed into a retirement of ease. They decided they couldn't give up the Barn and all that the theatre had begun to mean; not only to them.

One result of excavating to put in the new septic tank in the north paddock was the presence of bulldozers and the opportunity to level off the whole area. And it was over this flat area that the Barn funds paid to put down 'grass-reinforcing' netting. This pegged down mesh of tough netting settles in a half inch or so below the grass surface and in soft weather prevents any car from getting at all bogged down. No need now for the straw. One found out, by talking with the genial gent who supervised its laying down, that it came from the Dorset coast and was in fact the same tough mesh now used for trawlers' nets. And thereby hangs a touching tale.

We were approaching a production in which *fishing net* was the key element in the setting. James – having now learned the arts of casual acquisition from John the carpenter – brought the matter up with the man of getting some extra pieces; to be paid for, of course. Not a bit of it. The man liked these Barn blokes and what they were doing. The requisite amount – about the area of a large seine net – would arrive, free gratis.

What was it for – a play?
Yes, the fish nets in a play about Andrew, the saint, the fisherman . . .
Oh –
. . . who was martyred in Greece and, according to the play on the St Andrews type cross of the end timbers of the sort of racks for drying the nets. My wife and I saw these in Amalfi – Italy where his "remains" are.
Oh –
But he wasn't martyred there.
No – you said in Greece, didn't you. Where?
In Corinth.

47

The man looked strangely at James, and then at the net some of which he'd promised for the play.

I lost my wife recently. She was from Corinth. I'll see you get the net.

Something was working for us. What could James say? – except invite the bereaved man and hope that he'd come; and that the play would be something special for him. He never came (maybe Corinth was too sensitive a setting for him) but the net came. The net rack was built with its great St. Andrew's X end. All the sands of Corinth were Sussex sand barrowed into the Barn on sunny days, laid as a 'shore' from the Deck as 'sea' and on up the shelving Slope; and lit from gold to blood red on the day.

This *was* an *event*: a festival event; billed as *The Festival of the Four*; the four patron saints of the British Isles: *Andrew*, for Scotland – the *fisherman* of Galilee; *George*, for England – the *soldier* of Rome's empire; *Patrick*, for Ireland – the *shepherd* and priest; and *David*, for Wales – the *monk* and founder of an order. Four fifty-minute plays of which *Andrew* and *George* could be seen in the afternoon and *Patrick* and *David* in the evening. Or those who wanted to see what all four added up to – which was the evolution of the primitive Christian order on which our Western civilisation grew – could take a meal in a marquee in the Barn yard and see the lot on one day. A woman in the yard in the sun said to me, 'This is the Glyndebourne of Drama'. I bet that she didn't keep the comparison accurate by putting £10 twice into the collecting basket!

Three women – black and American – came starry eyed stumbling out of the Barn at the end, throwing their arms around Louise cried, 'Chile! how can we ever tell them back home what happened here?' It *was* quite an event in which the Barn reserves, human and physical, were stretched to the limit; stretched in fact a bit too far to keep the level of performance in several of the lesser roles up to the standards we'd begun to expect.

There were 88 parts with a company of 32 players. Backstage, Louise could be seen consulting her wallchart of Entrances and Exits with Stage Management and doing as much traffic control of persons on the move as when she was resettling displaced Ukranians, Hungarians, Poles and Greeks in post-war Munich.

It was this dropping of standards that encouraged James to institute before the next production a series of lecture-demonstrations in the Barn on the Arts of Theatre, planning and presenting them himself but using other professional players to demonstrate, eg: Character Creation, Handling of Costumes, Props and study of scripts etc. These were called Instructional Rehearsals, and as the last item of every session, a scene from the play in preparation was rehearsed by the company players with attendant professional player comment. The playing company was obliged to attend and the Friends of The Barn could come and watch as interest lectures.

In themselves they were a welcome success and their effect on the next, and major, production was so notably good that perhaps, artistically, this was the best production we ever did. The play *Adelaise*, had been done first as a radio play commissioned by the BBC for the 1951 Festival of Britain and as a stage play had been done out of town in Ashburton, Devon, but never in London or New York. *Adelaise*, about the young second wife and queen of Henry The First of England, and set in and around Arundel in Sussex, was our Jubilee Year summer production, 1977.

Perhaps because of the extra preparation of the Instructional Rehearsals and the unusual fact of the long period of rehearsals – with the whole holiday break of August in 'the pregnancy' of that play's production (we brought it to birth in October) – there was an unusually mature bringing together of Sight, Light, Sound and Touch, an unusual integrity in Costume, Lighting, Sound and Playing.

In this case costumes were designed by a talented young London artist – Friend of The Barn, and of the Forsyths' – Catherine Grubb. And it wasn't just in the settings of the play – from the great fireplace in the castle of Arundel to the shore by the mouth of the Arun – but in the action and text of the play that it was so at home in the sort of Theatre of Imagination the Barn had become. There was a belief of this playwright which I remember remarked upon by the actress wife of Bernard Miles when James was visiting the Mermaid Theatre during its construction: that he saw the stage as simply a standpoint from which the player could in all directions (including the auditorium) create by his speech and action a whole world of the play well beyond the walls of the theatre; that for the audience the player was a sort of reflector of a stage setting which extended to infinity. Eg, our audience were convinced that the on-stage wharfage and ropes leading to our Henhouse exit extended to, shore, ship and the whole sea at least as far as Normandy.

Beyond what was a peak of achievement of a Theatre now physically 'all there', the Barn had three further 'world premiers' in what had become a pattern in its annual programme of four events: Music in May, Summer Play and Winter Production, with occasionally a special Music or Music and Words event in Autumn.

It is interesting to note that one of the cohesive factors in the Barn's complement of players, production team, workers and helpers generally was the recruitment of the talent of whole families. I can think of eight families who had four of their members active over most of ten years and twelve families who had three.

The Forsytes' Barn, Ansty – 1977
(The Audience's View)

James Forsyth

CHAPTER FIVE

If we now recall how it all began, with that bit of perishing and primitive drama in the chill draughts of New Year's Eve 1971–72 – *The Masque of the Death and Re-birth of The Year* – then the Barn can be seen to be going into its sixth year. And, as the Drama in The Forsyths' Barn Theatre begins to be very much a personal drama in the life of the Forsyths, let me totally revert to the first person singular and be again story-teller direct.

Early in this year – 1978 – our small Policy Group of nine, including our two selves were sitting around the old octagonal table in the 'undercroft' of Grainloft; the low ceiling above us of oak beams and boards the gentle colour of a jersey cow. I repeated what I had just said, because none of the faithful seven present was prepared to believe me, '*seven years will be a good and adequate life for a venture like this.*' Fully aware – as we now all were – that The Forsyths' Barn Theatre had become somewhat of a local institution and a matter of community pride, I still maintained – and still do – that once any human institution, large or small, begins to exist simply to perpetuate itself, rather than serve the purpose it was created for, then if it isn't on its way out it should be.

It seemed to me there were signs, in our planning anxieties, that we were beginning to be concerned simply to keep it going. Provided that for a year or two we maintained, or improved upon, the standards we had reached with *Adelaise* then the Barn would, to my mind, have achieved its purpose as Theatre; and for an adequate number of years. However, that something so patently successful should stop at all! This seemed quite senseless; especially to those who most enjoyed its productions and were least aware of the toll taken in time, energy and health, on the inevitably small band of the faithful few who bore – and always will bear – the main burden, artistic and administrative, in such voluntary ventures.

Privately, I was all too aware of the serious strain on that DIY disciplinarian whose standards of Administration were stoically high and whose reluctance to delegate work was incurable, yet who would never give up while the work was there – Louise. The diminishing distance between eyes and the text to be typed now presaged in any case an early end to any improvement of sight through any improvement of glasses. (Two cataract operations would soon become necessary.)

Though I was just a novice OAP Louise was five years ahead of me;

51

a fact, denied by her appearance and vitality; and of which only I was aware. What I was not aware of, or prepared for was the rapidly developing personal tragedy, that was to bring to an end our greatly good marriage and with it the life of The Forsyths' Barn Theatre.

At this Policy Group meeting in 1978 I was simply fighting for a bit more leisure time for Louise, also more time for myself to write. But in any case, a time had to come when we would not have the resources nor the energy to continue. One of the hallmarks of the whole venture had been that it was not in the hands of the rash and the young but, well . . . let's say, the mad and mature. By going much beyond seven years the natural wastage by age, illness and the movement of some of our stalwarts to retiral areas further West and cheaper, would inevitably lose us some of the most tried, trained and mature members of our company. That would mean having to train, in our eccentric and demanding ways, new young blood. More time and energy.

Whatever was then decided about the years ahead, our next play production decidedly *would not* be our last. This was *N For Napoleone*, a new play about the Buonaparte family. With 'any other business' now ticked off the list of her clearly typed Agenda and Louise gone next door to bring in not hot punch but hot coffee, I should perhaps complete your picture of the Policy Group and emphasise its nature by giving due credit to four members of it hardly noted so far.

Our principal player who sat on the Policy Group for most of our years was a Management Consultant whose head was cool and whose heart was in the countryside. He worked from home; which was one of the mill cottages. I, with my dog, would meet Jerry Walls on the early morning walks, moving along the hedge-rows with his faithful terrier, quietly wonder-struck by the wildflowers he was collecting; and sometimes audibly learning his part while on the move under the sky, before he circled back down to the Mill and the statistical charts on his drawing board (and to his forceful wife Peggi, who was both a player and a producer at the Barn). Another calm and faithful member of great good humour was a Council Roads and Highways Officer and Engineer. He ran the Sound for productions. Derek Gee had the excellently cool and unflappable temperament anyone needs in that job; completely consistent with the fact that he was a keen rock climber. The regular lady member of the group was Rosemary Garforth, whose devotion to duty made it almost impossible to get her to accept a relief 'Props Girl' (to dispense props to players during one run of the play) so that she could join the audience and see the results of her work. She was the wife of Major Bill Garforth and, as with at least seven other established local families, the Garforth commitment to the Barn became a family affair, involving sons and daughters as players and technicians.

Then there was Dick 2 – Dick 1 being the already mentioned Dick Walker. Dick Doyle was a senior architect to the Southern Railway, and sometimes a player, but more significantly for us the one who designed and built the players' gallery of old timbers at the upstage end, first required for *The Festival of The Four*. Straddled across a beam eight feet above the soft sandstone with a mallet and wood chisel in his hand, Dick was heard to say – in a sort of builder's bliss – 'I feel as the medieval builders of our ancient cathedrals must have felt when they got above the stonework on to the timbering.' Our other architect, succeeding Jerry both as a principal player and Policy Group Member, was Peter Searl, a strong convivial character of great good humour with a natural gift for the player's art. Besides playing a heart-breaking St Andrew, he could be relied upon to relieve the tyranny of rehearsals with off-stage humour; as when in the play about that tyrant Buonaparte the off-stage clamour of the crowd included, 'James for First Consul!'.

Final regular beyond the first two years was Tony Hill, who, having become our nearest neighbour by buying Old Place, was invited in out of courtesy and to enjoy the peace of mind of knowing what went on next door when the Cabal got round that old octagonal table. He dealt in antiques, printing and other things.

The intention to produce the Buonaparte family play was announced: rehearsals to start in April, performances July. Invitations went out from Louise's duplicator. It was now called *N For Napoleone*, the 'N' being for the famous and infamous French Emperor and the 'e' of the italianate spelling of 'Buonaparte' for the Corsican he always was, native of that passionate island where dwell 'the Irish of the Mediterranean'. Which brings up the business of our –

CHOICE OF PLAYS

In order to make any sense at all of 'playwright's workshop theatre' and set the benefit of 'bench-testing' certain plays against the steady financial drain of months of non-earning work on my part, the repertoire of the Barn had to be mostly Forsyth new plays. This one had started life under another title and as an idea for TV and had already had a fascinating, if frustrating, history. This demonstrates an interesting contrast between the Barn and the Profession.

After unusual success on TV with the patron saints plays, *Four Triumphant* in 1968, and the Tolstoy play *The Last Journey* in 1972, Cecil Clarke, Head of Drama at ATV (who had been Stage Director in the early days when the Old Vic did my play on Villon – *The Other Heart*) commissioned me to write a 'major TV play about any famous character in History'.

I had recently read Butterfield's brilliant little book on Napoleon: a character regarded till then by most of my generation, and by me, as a dictator hardly less suspect than Hitler. In it I saw startling signs of the very personal passion of this great native of the island of Corsica – and then discovered that Josephine – the girl from the island of Martinique – was a far more complex and important character than I had ever imagined her to be. When I had read into the life of Letitia, Napoleon's mother, that other monumentally important woman in his life, I was gripped by this set of characters. I chose Napoleon as my 'famous character in History'. It was to be a full-length TV play to follow after Terence Rattigan's *Nelson*.

Well – I was no Abel Gance, but I began to see, after Louise and I had done research in Paris and Corsica, that what I was working on was not *one* TV play but more properly a series of *three*. On seeing the draft scripts Cecil Clarke agreed. But, as ATV could not at that time consider such a series they, with exceptional generosity, released the scripts so that I might offer them to BBC TV. The BBC said thank you, no. So – I was stuck with a major bit of writing for TV and nobody to blame but myself; and perhaps Buonaparte, for having lived such a large-scale life.

The material lay in limbo for a time. Then one day we went to Oxford; to see an old colleague, Alan Badel, play the part of Edmund Kean in Jean Paul Sartre's stage play *Kean*: an absolutely brilliant performance. Here was an actor who could play all the 'N' of Napoleone, had French blood in his veins and was as passionate as a Corsican. We had supper afterwards, only to find that his wife Yvonne was wearing a favourite pendant about her neck – of Napoleon! 'Send us the play.' We did. We sent them the script – of the TV 3. Both 'went over the moon' about it and 'the *passion* of it!' was their response. It was at that point I decided to do the dangerous thing: wright – because, I repeat, plays are not written but wrought from a number of arts, not just the writer's – a play for a particular star player. Alan's star was certainly in the ascendant when *Kean* transferred to London's West End. We went to see it again. He was as impressive as ever; though his voice did not seem to be standing up to the strain of the run.

Having wrought from the material what I thought was an effective and theatrical way to mould the TV three into the form of a single stage play, I went eagerly to work. Surprisingly soon, and happy with the result, we sent the play to him.

It's a temperamental world, the world of Theatre. Something happened never quite explained. Alan couldn't be contacted and, when he was, he was slightly incoherent, said on the phone it was because of his mother (to whom he was probably as attached as Napoleon to Letitia) – his mother was 'ill – dying, in poverty'. It sounded melodramatic; more like Edmund Kean speaking. But his distress seemed very real. I knew that there was this trouble with his voice, which *could* make the idea of playing a run of any play an intolerable prospect. What if it were cancer his mother was dying of? . . . what if he feared, he himself? the throat? . . . I didn't know, I don't know now – but he dropped all interest in the play so brutally I was too bitter to find out. Then some months later, he called me to say that he was going to form his own *TV* company! – that there would be more money in it for us both. Would I consider re-writing my play for TV? Lord!! I was now fully committed to a passionate belief in my play as a full length Theatre play. To go back on this? I was now the Scot less rational and more passionate than any Corsican. No! With a feeling not short of betrayal, I said to hell with Money, the Big Time, TV *and* star actors. My play was going forward to the Theatre. And in a little while it seemed to be so – to an Edinburgh Festival production. Then this plan too hit money troubles on the management side, and collapsed. At that point it finally became, for me, to blazes with the commercial and so-called 'professional' theatre of the whole bloody Entertainments Industry. Back to the Barn, 'Playwright's Workshop' and the Arts of Theatre unencumbered. And here ends the history of that particular frustration and some of the perils of the profession of playwright. For we went ahead to produce the play with no star in the Barn and with real success; the only true success in Theatre being love for the play by those it is played to. It's a shared business, with no sure fire recipe for success.

Not that there weren't problems in Ansty too; artistic problems. *Casting* a Napoleon! And the *setting*! Think of it! The whole rough rustic atmosphere of the Barn, which had so naturally suited a 'country' play like *She Stoops To Conquer*, the peasant quality of *Emmanuel*, and Early English *Adelaise*, how could we get it to convey the more sophisticated settings of *'N' For Napoleone*? of 'No. 6 Rue Chantereine, Paris' – house of Josephine? even 'a bedchamber in the palace of The Tuileries'?? And we could have problems too in *Costume*. Because it was what the profession called a 'costume play' with several uniforms (of high Napoleonic rank too), also women's court dresses of the Empire style. In the time available, *could* we make all our own costumes for this play? For, if we had to hire some – the cost! And what a defeat in our battle to originate everything on the spot. Well (if you are anxious) see pictures between pages 44 and 45. Time and a minor mutiny led by the leader of the Costumemakers, Louise, forced us to hire three uniforms, but all the rest shown there were Barn creations.

The *Casting* problem was met and solved too. We had never, as you now know, consciously formed A Company. But by this time, within the qualifying catchment area (of a radius of 1 hour's travelling time from the Barn) there would be about 60 players ready and anxious to play in a Barn production if work and home circumstances allowed them time. For, the reputation of the Barn had come to be that its standards were 'professional'. Of about 20 of these potential players one could think of now as fully 'professed to Theatre' and a cut above good amateur talent; four perhaps would actually have had professional experience. You could add to the willing and ready, with some Barn experience behind them, about 45 men, women and youngsters skilled in one area of Costumes, Props, Sets, Lighting, Stage Management and about 30 'helpers on the day'. And it may be of interest to know that, from its eleven years, 6 young players went on and into the professional theatre, TV, or showbusiness.

In casting for the part of Napoleon we couldn't have a Badel, and this play wouldn't work with a player of no authority in the principal role; nor one however authoritative – who was seven feet tall, four wide and was a blue eyed Nordic; not even if he stuck his hand behind his waistcoat buttons and brooded!

Fortunately, one of our players – the LAMDA trained and now local teacher Geoffrey Robertson – was not too tall, was dark, handsome in what could be an Italian way; and had the authority of a keen intelligence. Also he *might* be available. He *was* – on most dates required. Our rehearsals anyway were always a strange patchwork of availability. Where you cannot, as in the professional theatre, command a player's whole daytime working hours you have to have this patchwork, or jig-saw schedule of rehearsal and make it run over a rather extended time. Not less than three months as opposed to the profession's concentrated few weeks. But gestation, anyway, needs time.

We had excellent casting possibilities for the women's roles of Josephine and her daughter, Hortense; and Letitia and daughter Pauline. Good supporting roles, like General Junot, were no problem but it could be that the approach to rehearsals of this play meant persisting anxiety about the available quality of support acting at the fringes. It was a cast of 11. Anyway, we organised once again – on the then popular Master Class principal –

A PROGRAMME OF INSTRUCTIONAL REHEARSALS
These were to fit into the first sessions of normal rehearsals starting in April – and to involve Company (Players and Production Team) and, again, Friends of the Barn as guests. We continued thereafter into the full Company rehearsal schedule of 25 to 30 periods of not less than $1\frac{1}{2}$ hours duration (mostly Wednesday and Friday evenings 7.30 to 10.30 pm), covering almost four months.

The 1977 hand-out to Company and Friends of the Barn had read, and still applied now –

EACH SESSION will consist of a talk on the subject (e.g. *"The Designer's Part"*) plus an element of practical rehearsal and demonstration, using members of the Barn Company.

SOME SESSIONS will involve professional specialists in the particular subject. The hope again was:

that this will heighten appreciation from audience and improve performance from players and company.

Not to seem too serious, it is also expected that discussion will be stimulated and some fun be had on the way.

Sessions will normally last for an hour and a half but playing members will sometimes be required to stay on till 10 o'clock for practical rehearsal. Others will be welcome to stay on and watch if they wish.

FEE: 50p per session for Barn Company Members: £1 per session for others.

Some fee was necessary to pay for guest professionals brought in and, in this case, something for my work in preparation of the whole scheme. It was hard going. *But*, for *Adelaise* the evidence had been that it was worthwhile.

One out of the many letters of congratulations that we had received at that time is worth quoting here.

'Last Sunday afternoon my wife and I visited your Theatre . . . and were treated to a feast of dramatic art which we have not seen surpassed by any professional cast. The eloquence of the dialogue, the atmosphere of drama, and the simplicity of the setting created so much impact and left us spellbound to *Adelaise* and the surroundings in which it was performed.'

We had, none of us, any wish for those standards to drop. The 1978 Schedule of *Instructional Rehearsals* read:

1. THE CREATION OF CHARACTER
   a) by the Playwright on the page.
   b) by the Player on the stage.

2. THE ARTS OF SPEECH IN THE CREATION OF CHARACTER
   The Written Word to the Spoken Word.

3. SPEECH AND MOVEMENT – COSTUME AND CHARACTER
   Excerpts from scenes of different styles.

4. ENSEMBLE ACTING AND THE INTER-ACTION OF CHARACTER UPON CHARACTER

5. SPEECH AND ITS RELATION TO THE OTHER ARTS OF THE THEATRE WITH SPECIAL REFERENCE TO SETTING AND DESIGN

6. RHYTHM, PACE AND 'THE MUSIC' OF THE PLAYING

7. FROM A SHOUT TO A WHISPER
Performance and criticism of a scene in rehearsal for the Summer Production.

With all this to get on the go, the planning of the annual *Music in May* (with its usual seasonable prologue of the children in costumes doing their Spring dance around the be-ribboned maypole on the Barn Green); painting and etching for an exhibition in the Autumn; writing of a radio play, you can assess the state of idleness around the Forsyth homestead. What chance for Louise of 'more leisure' now?

But – by-passing what was a happy, but showery *Music in May* – let's take *N for Napoleone* to its conclusion and make a point on the way about the convention of scene-setting and scene-change in The Barn. Ours was, as you know, no neutral playing space (like the 'black box' or characterless empty space of most modern 'studio' theatres.) It had a character from the beginning, a character and atmosphere in which players and those played with and to – the audience – were *both* embraced by the surround of these old wooden walls and the run of the great roof timbers above. We accepted this likeable ambience, never tried to give another character to or 'argue with the walls'. But within the playing area we always designed things to *work from the centre out*; *and* in this order of importance:

1) *The Player* as character.
2) *The Costume,* containing and being his or her "skin" for the particular play.
3) *The Props* handled, and played with, by the player.
4) *Scenic or Set Elements* evocative of the place in which the player's action took place.
5) *The Atmosphere* of the action. The sort of water the fish needs to swim in (and dies a dry death without): mostly a matter of lighting, maybe music and
6) *The Environment* which is the whole extension to infinity off-stage of the world of, the play.

But, in working out the Settings for 'N' I decided on a sort of heresy. For the first time I *would* 'argue with the walls': but only with token *panels* sufficient in area and visual effect for the audience to play their part in completing, in their imagination, the final 'furnishing' of settings. In this play we had, twice at least, to suggest an enclosed and sophisticated space. These *panels* were five in number and of heavy plywood, 6×2 feet in size, which could hang upright between the old oak uprights of the walls and be easily reversed on their hangings to show a second side, by one swift lift and turn of an adept stagehand.

One side of the panel was a dull, grenadier red, with a huge 'N', plus a laurel wreath for victory and the Buonaparte family symbol of the bee (also imperial eagle). The other side was pale blue with elegant white strips running vertically. The red side with its commanding 'N' was used in the military and imperial scenes; the other used to take us into the atmosphere of Josephine's house in Paris. And, having touched the walls, I touched the Barn floor too; and reinforced the sense of feminine interior with easily removable, easily setable, runners and rug-size sections of faded blue carpet. These were painted in a delicate imperial design with whiting and glue-size. (One of the many deft pieces of artistry of Rosemary Keith.) In a playing area which was always seen from above by the audience upon our stepped seating, the floor was quite a compelling part of the Barn settings (remember the original 'grave'!) Usually limited to the neutrality of old boards of Deck or Rostrum in character with the Barn walls, or the natural earth of the Slope, it was partly altered for the scene in which Napoleon's campaign tent is set by 'the shore at Aboukir', by *sand* – barrowloads of it brought in on a dry Summer Sunday afternoon to transform a section of the playing area. This helped 'transport' us to Egypt!

Two set elements more or less by themselves announced to the audience the presence or impending presence in any scene of either Napoleon or his 'Madame Mère', Letitia. One was immovably a part of the fixed settings. This was a pavilion-like canvas *tent*, striped pale blue and white (like the reverse side of the wall panels). It sat in an up-stage corner of the playing area on a dais built up not of wood but of Sussex clay modelled to shape and pounded into a firm platform. (The way we did this sort of thing or carved out levels of the soft sandstone slope sometimes made our staging of the playing area a department of Sculpture not Carpentry.) The other was a movable masterpiece carpentered by our invaluable back-stage consultant who had been stage carpenter at the Old Vic – John Terry. This was the old, black sedan chair of Letitia Buonaparte, in the original of which Napoleon had nearly been born (like premature birth in a taxi today!). In the Corsican original they had run pregnant Mama Buonaparte back to the house in a hurry, from prayer in the cathedral in Ajaccio. The pregnancy ended and the little person's great life began just inside the street door; so they say. More like a meaningful piece of sculpture than a dark piece of furniture for a set scene, this would be the key piece for several of Letitia's scenes: splendid to play around, into and out of.

The tent served not only to be the campaign tent and HQ of General Buonaparte but it also became the tented bed in Josephine's house in Paris. Because she had, as a matter of historical fact, canopied their marital bed like a tent because, as she said, 'wherever Napoleone rests must be the headquarters of the world'. And when our striped tent served for the imperial bed in the palace of the Tuileries, we simply revealed its silk lining and bordered it by the panels with the Imperial

'N', then hedged it about on either side by the colourful battle standard captured within the scene at Aboukir. For final palatial glory we dropped in on top of it (by a wire run down from a tie beam) a grand fleur de lys crown; metalwork of a fine Props department artist, Bert Wells, a builder and talented amateur artist.

THE SCENE-CHANGES

This multiple use within one play of set units almost heraldic, or emblematic, in their use was typical of Barn productions. And in their manipulation to achieve scene-change the drill was this:– light would fade from previous scene, and as a dim light of one colour suffused the whole playing-area (for *Napoleone* red, for *Adelaise* steel blue) and, with Music or a Sound Effect to cover the scene-change, eg Distant Gunfire, the stage crew under their i/c David, would come on dressed in the uniform of their hessian tabards. Deftly as possible, without rush (but rehearsed and timed to the minute) they would set, re-set or remove the elements of the setting, in full view of the audience. And the audience came to expect and enjoy this 'play' between scenes of the play which, when it went as planned, was designed to be part and parcel of the whole rhythm of the play.

With our comparatively large playing area and its different levels, and Gallery, we had little difficulty – and no expense – in accommodating six different settings in this one play. We had a sort of Shakespearean freedom of location and with a switch of focus of attention we were able to flow from one scene-setting to another.

Costume did give us headaches; and heartaches. Even with Louise and eight of her costume-creating ladies working full out, we did hire, from Fox's of Covent Garden, three back-up uniforms. But Louise herself insisted on tackling the carefully tailored uniform of her favourite Barn player, playing Napoleone. The women, beautifully costumed to our original designs appeared in elegant Barn creations.

The extraordinary devotion Louise gave, in time and care, to the costume of Napoleon on top of all the administrative work she had to do, of invitations, tickets, the editing and printing of the programmes etc, can now be seen to be the beginnings of dangerous stress and strain.

Rehearsals went well and, from the Wednesday First Night onward the play played so that the audiences were gripped and applause was loud and sustained. But as evidence of audience reaction from someone experienced to know a theatrical hawk from a handsaw, let me briefly tell you the reaction of the actor Edward Fox when he came to see the play.

His family being Sussex neighbours, we had watched Edward develop right from the days he did a Chekhov one-acter in a Hoxton hall with a group of young associates including Sarah Miles. But at this time he was filming for TV in the part of Edward, in the Edward VII/Mrs Simpson epic. However, he did want to see the first half, up to the interval. He had 'to be back in London and up at dawn' for filming. Pity – but fair enough. His was a major professional commitment, with everything at stake, in career, cash etc. However, as an interest for the company, and a bit of the supposed glamour of stardom, I asked him, and he willingly agreed, to look into the Dressing Room at half time and, before he took off, to say hello to the cast. His visit was to one of the final performances and previous audience reaction argued against him not liking the play at all; for if that were so it would be awkward for him to go 'backstage'. He came out of the Barn at the interval with quite a strained look on his face. This could be the product of being too polite to say how bad he felt it all was. And his 'marvellous' and chatty remarks to the cast, could easily be the old dressing room dilemma of wondering how not to say nothing but not to hurt either. However, he *has* a gift for looking withdrawn; abstracted. The Interval over, I rang the handbell happily around the yards (and the loos) to summon and shepherd the audience in for the second half (my one bit of Public Relations on the day and a thing I always loved doing loud and clear). I had started the whole thing with a sheep bell in my hand, hadn't I? And a Scottish Shepherd was in my family tree. With the audience shepherded in, I then sought him and arranged for Edward's departure. 'No, no. Don't want to go; not yet.' So Louise and I arranged to get him back in on the front of the seating next to the exit; so that he might slip out and away very soon. The play re-started and I sat next to him. From time to time I glanced at my wristwatch; and at his face. For whatever reason this was the face of a rapt man. But when most of an hour had gone I tapped the watch and whispered, 'Edward, almost ten o'clock.' He brushed the warning aside and didn't take his attention off the play. Still later, and well beyond his 'deadlines', I anxiously whispered, 'Coming up to 10.30 and –' 'Won't go.' He brushed it aside, and I gave up. This now seemed to me like a man of the professional theatre saying at heart what I had said, 'To hell with the Big Time, Stage and TV, this is what it was all about – rough or ready Theatre, but the Art.' He not only stayed till the end, he stayed on to discuss the whole thing with great enthusiasm, before we sent him on his way through the night to London with some food and refreshment in him: perhaps 'nourished' in the best of both senses?

And if between eight and nine hundred people had been down the lane to the event – which they had – and had seen the play well played, what more did one want? Nothing. Except a bit more rest; and a bit more money. For the latter we had to start (without much of the former) to prepare for an Exhibition of my Paintings. For this, as usual, we transformed and specially lit the two white-walled cowsheds backstage, to make them a sort of Summer Gallery.

And if, from this point on, the story of the Forsyths' Barn Theatre merges fully and inextricably with the personal drama of the Forsyths, it will have to be hoped that, in the centre section of the story, I have sufficiently shown that whatever the efforts on our part nothing could have been done in its fullness without the many who came and worked with us for nothing but the sheer love of the thing and notably the several stagehands, construction gangs and costume-makers not named here.

Louise, the perfectionist, had, in the making of the Napoleon costumes, worked far too hard for far too many hours on top of all the work done by her on Invitations, Tickets, Programmes and other things on the Admin side. And with the Exhibition of my drawings, etchings and paintings following much too close she still insisted that in the usual transformation of cowsheds into Exhibition Galleries, the Number One Gallery, the 'Prom' needed a whole repainting of the old brick walls. This in the last of the Summer days, she did almost entirely single-handed while I was struggling to complete the acid bath 'biting' of the latest etching without gassing myself with the fumes. (The wash cubicle at the end of the other cowshed, the 'Dressing Room' was annually transformed by me into an Etching Studio.) After hours of slapping white paint on the walls, Louise, quite naturally complained of an ache in her overworked right arm. We soldiered on and the Exhibition was a gratifying success, putting some cash in the bank account in the golden Autumn. We were then involved in preparation for the Christmas repeat production of *What The Dickens!* – the popular choice – when Louise mentioned 'a lump' near her right breast.

In what was part ignorance on my part, part egocentric obsession with the pressure of work, but now I see as almost criminal negligence, I paid no serious consideration to this quite casual announcement. It was only when she finally brought it to the notice of her niece that the latter immediately bundled her off to see the Doctor. She was quickly put in the hands of a Consultant Surgeon. Malignant Tumour of the right breast in an unfortunately advanced state was diagnosed. The need was for 'an urgent operation'.

CHAPTER SIX

It seemed Louise had suppressed the fact for some considerable time, strictly forbidding anyone else to tell me until *Napoleone* was over. The specialist's insistence on urgency, and the pain in the right arm, were very frightening. Within days, in Brighton, she was operated on. Sick with anxiety and hurrying down to see her at the first opportunity I backed out of our garage on the usual curve and swung straight into a visiting van. Her niece on her first visit had also a minor crash on the way to the hospital. Two signs of the state of anxiety at this time. But, in most skilful of hands, that all too common operation on women, mastectomy, was carried out. It was a success: if one can equate 'success' with the trauma to any sensitive woman of the removal of a dear breast.

She recovered well. Anxiety diminished. She was in great spirits. Work towards the Christmas 1978 production went forward while we all conspired to reduce her involvement to nil. In the end, at the end of the play, the warmth and festivity of Dickens's Dingley Dell Christmas Party spread out from the Barn and up into 'Grainloft', making a thankful Christmas time of rest; with a potentially happy New Year ahead. Apart from some nagging anxiety that the enemy had been engaged rather late in the day, all seemed well and we planned ahead for 1979, but reducing the amount of work for Louise. I also reduced the Barn work for myself; for it was impossible to keep Louise out of it if I was in it. The astrological faithful would say we were so twinned together because we were both born under the same sign, of Pisces, only one day apart on the calendar. The zodiacal sign certainly was a faithful signature of how we behaved. The individual independence and passionate arguments were true to the fact that the two fishes swam in different directions but were always, as were we, inseparably in the swim together; all times, all weathers. Love, where it deserves a capital 'L' is a tough, and not passive, concept.

The plan was to hand over total responsibility for the now annual celebration of *Music in May* to Howard Blake. He was still resident two fields away, at the old water mill, and welcomed the opportunity to meet general demand for another production of his witty one-act opera, *The Station*. I would do no Summer Production this year. Geoffrey Robertson, who had so successfully played Napoleon and had – besides his training at LAMDA – had considerable experience of amateur production, would produce a bill in July of the three Chekhov one-acters, *The Bear*, *The Wedding* and *The Anniversary*, together with a

Chekhov comic monologue delivered by Jerry. Louise was still in any case, having to deal with the tiresome added business of allowing the cataract of the eyes to get worse before anything could be made better. I note that it was around this time that I was getting fascinated by a new subject for a play – no – two subjects at once. It wasn't the reason for writing it, but, I also note, that the central character in the one play performed a successful cataract operation on his own beloved Mother! – José Rizal, the Filipino patriot. Neither subject could give me any assurance of being with any immediacy income-making projects, so I went on anyway painting, drawing and etching to produce works for another Exhibition, the others having been patently rewarding.

My form of occupational schizophrenia, between the Artist I was first trained to be and the Playwright that life had made of me, was plaguing me again. There were at least two good reasons why over-burdened Louise was all in favour of the Playwright now making way *entirely* for the Artist. I had with most plays so obviously had to fight every inch of the way to get the work beyond the wrighting and into production. With the paintings and other pictures appreciation seemed to be immediate and sales followed closely behind. The playwright's art was not a DIY medium – it depended on so many other people and their talents to make it work, and she was a great advocate of independence and Do It Yourself. And, she was against the second play's subject anyway.

This subject arose from the re-reading of a letter my father had once written to me, from Scotland in the years shortly before his death. It referred – the letter – to that 'grand biblical poem, the Book of Ruth'.

Would I not, he had written, consider writing a play on this theme, of the young woman who had 'stood among the alien corn' and for love and fidelity had said, 'my people will be your people; my god your god' and would I then think please of 'our dear Louise' – who in marrying me had moved out of her sphere of social service and the rescue of hundreds of the war's refugees and into the alien sphere of the Theatre and the Arts? Louise knew, unfortunately about this letter, and when I brought the Ruth subject up thought that I was directly equating her with the legendary young lady who, to her mind, was probably as seductive as Naomi was panderous and old Boaz lecherous. No. She was *not for* the subject. Neither had I been till now not wanting to do 'a biblical play'. But coming across the letter I had again looked at 'the book of the play', and had seen *Ruth* suddenly as both a refugee story and an Arab/Israeli story too: Jews of Bethlehem dealing with Arab refugees from Moab. I secretly decided I was going to do it. Louise secretly decided it wasn't going to be done. This wasn't a time for one of the passionate, but stressful arguments. It was a natural subject for the Barn, but it was a summer subject anyway and with all we had in hand, together with Louise's first cataract operation, spring and summer 1979 saw the Barn going forward in other good hands.

Howard Blake's bright, witty and fully professional attack gave *The Station* a production that was a spring joy, applauded by all the Friends of the Barn, and in July the four items of Chekhov were reduced to three (for reasons of casting *The Anniversary* dropped out). But, because of this gap in the total Chekhov bill of fare, we brought in – as a sort of entre-acte entertainment and also an integral element of the celebrations in *The Wedding* – some Russian folk dance. By good fortune the local dance school were at that time studying, with its senior grade of dance pupils, *Russian* Folk Dance! The Barn wardrobe helped to improve the costume of three of their dancers and they improved our production with a delightful and meaningful addition in dance. This had amazingly happy consequence when we came to Ruth, as we did; but of that happy consequence later.

This October the first of two cataract operations were performed. From the word Go this was a success of a quite unqualified kind. Even before the possibility of wearing any lens or new glasses (it would be contact lenses) colour and light came back to her and flooded into her life. The result was thrilling to her and a delight to watch. It was not unlike seeing a withering plant grow back to total vitality. It was a restoration not just of sight, of vision, but of total vitality. We stopped worrying about her health now except about the time it would take to get the other eye done.

That Autumn of 1979, with new heart we went ahead to prepare for the Winter production *Wenceslas*. However, we stopped promising it for Christmas, which would be too much pressure again, and I re-scheduled rehearsals to take us into the New Year, leading up to performance in February. With the Christmas holiday break this would mean a split rehearsal period again. But, by this, I hoped we might even gain, as we were surprised to do when in October 1977 we produced *Adelaise*. There was then a sort of maturing in all the processes of preparation, much of which must have been subconscious. The subconscious in any art being a very active business anyway.

One of the excitements that the audience never knew about producing *Wenceslas* was how a production by presumed amateur escapists seeming to do a play about a childish legend lodged in a Christmas carol, and staged in the back woods of Sussex, could suddenly seem to be a dangerous intrusion into contemporary world politics.

Ever since young Jan Palach burned himself to death in Wenceslas Square in Prague, as the ultimate in protest, and the people of what was old Bohemia suffered the armoured suppression of the 1968 Russian invasion – with its cold cruel imposition of the 'Prague Spring' – I had felt drawn to the subject. But now, in reading such history as there was on the reign and the death of Wenceslas, I was very struck by the parallels between the 1968 'Imperial' invasion of the Warsaw pact powers and the 10th Century invasion by the forces of the Franco/Germanic Empire. Both were tyrannically righteous powers one communist of a kind, one Christian of a kind. Dubchek had a similar dilemma and ultimatum to deal with as Wenceslas.

I was yet to know that my 'yonder peasant' would turn out to be no true peasant at all but a deadly decoy, leading saintly Wenceslas out 'on the feast of Stephen' to a martyr's death (an interpretation based upon the 10th Century politics at work within the Wenceslas family). I was, without much artistic licence at all, taking people imaginatively into the past in order to deal with a human drama now of immediate relevance to the present: a favourite game:

Having got the play into shape on the page it was my habit as Producer* to do several lone sessions of what I would call Dreaming and Scheming. This is the sort of thing any director of a play does, at home in his study or, if it's a high-powered production, in some quiet hotel 'away from it all'. Mine was done in the Barn where the event would be, either sitting with notebook up in the Auditorium imagining one's way through the whole action, or walking it out around the playing area; testing the production possibilities against the physical limitations and opportunities of the Barn.

After a few productions the old wooden barn became for me an instrument I could play; knowing what I could expect the audience's imagination to do, e.g. that with a certain light and element of token tree they would accept that the action was at sunset in the open; that with a bench and pair of old bellows and the play of a glow of reddish light we would be looking into a dying fire. 'We' because it was always a question of getting the audience to follow and be with it. That, given a *whiff* of mist, certain off-stage sounds, e.g. a horn sounded and referred to in the script as a guide to a ship in fog, we would be by the sea, and a ship off-shore.

During the Dreaming and Scheming phase of *Wenceslas* an unpredictable coincidence of wishes between us two Pisceans added an

---

*In the Barn one was back to the old label Producer rather than Director of the play (who today can too often be a specialist in directing actors assisted by other specialists in the other parts of the production as Lighting, Movement, Setting etc.) My commitment was all-arts, all departments, and on the day I was, I dare say, more like a football team manager, present on the bench, with his team in play; giving them the pep-talk before they prepared themselves to go on; keeping on-call in the interval and gearing each performance to the particular audience I had seen in. Some professional play directors feel that their job ends with the Dress Rehearsal.

unusual, but very effective, extra element to the Setting elements of the Barn. In working out the action of the play I wanted a high point in the playing area, a place from which Wenceslas and the Page would look out over snow covered Bohemia and see the distant figure of the 'peasant' away below. In the theatre of evoked imagination the best location for a landscape of snow is not on stage at all, but in the imagination of the audience. This scene would therefore be played right towards the auditorium and into the infinite landscape behind the many pairs of eyes there. Yet it was not the sort of intimate dialogue where Napoleone and Josephine, like two super cats had scented out their relationship. That scene had been played right down by the 'bulwark'. For this, on the other hand, the gallery was too far back, too physically removed from the audience. How could we get my pair of Wenceslas and Page, high up but close?

ENTER, FROM GRAINLOFT, THE BALCONY

In the conversion of our granary to 'Grainloft', a special architectural feature had been added to the south face of the little granary: a sort of loft-level outside balcony. To Louise, it had more to do with architectural affectation than rural domestic life. Besides, it set its two substantial timber legs right down in front of her big southern window in the undercroft: and the slatted deck of its upperworks shadowed her desk depressingly. It had to go, and – when she could prove that its attachment to the house let some rain seep in – orders were given for it to go.

As up at my loft and studio level it had offered me the opportunity to step out of a sort of French window and address the birds at tree-top level, she had anticipated opposition from the Artist. But no. This was exactly at the time when I was looking for that high point from which 'Good King Wenceslas' could 'look down'. This sort of rural pulpit on stilts was just the thing!

My willing co-conspirators, David Stredwick and his Stage Crew, man-handled the thing round and into the Barn. With a bit of additional stain, its already weathered timbers were rendered to be in complete harmony with the old timbers of the Barn. And with its legs dowelled into the downstage area of the Big Rostrum, stage right, the little slatted and be-railed floor this 'pulpit' gave me that high point for two players I had so desperately wanted. It sat near enough to the audience and about 12 feet above the Deck of the threshing floor. David and his henchmen then carpentered a slatted catwalk back to join with the up-stage Gallery. In the play, coldly spot-lit and isolated by 'outer darkness', the two players, plus the words of the play and the distant sound effect of the cry of a wolf, transformed the audience's imagination into a frozen white moonlit landscape. The so-called 'magic of the theatre': but no trick, just a sympathetic sharing of imaginations by the old compact of 'let's play'. – 'Let's make-believe' tends to be illusionist, tricksy theatre. Anyway, our house's loss was the Theatre's gain and it worked. For producer it offered the added excitement of the two players – King and Page – being able to start this scene in a warm glow of an imagined dying fire right down by the 'bulwark', two feet from the front row, and to travel, as they played the scene, up the earth slope onto the stage left rostrum, up the stairs which led up to the Gallery and then right along its backstage length coming finally on out to our architectural pulpit, which was now accepted as a vantage point in the castle high above the River Vltava, as it wound its way round the castle rock back towards Prague.

Like most set elements, the Balcony served more than a double purpose within the one production. In this production, with an onion-shaped, Slav cupola crowning the pulpit, its porch-like pillared shape became the entrance to the forest chapel where Wenceslas was lured to his death. And again, with Cupola removed it became the porched entrance to a barn where choirs of Slovak locals were in contest in a Harvest Festival competition with a choir of the Germanic occupation troops. Which all sounds lavish, but is simply a richness of texture from the use of all Theatre arts and crafts; and craftyness. In our case all costing little in cash; lots in effort and invention. This new element of our Setting we called the Balcony; to distinguish it from the sort of Minstrel's Gallery which we had earlier constructed to run along the back wall, fully up-stage.

Playing with those elements of set – which became recognizable pieces to our regular audience – was all in accord with the sense of invitation to them, imaginatively, to join us in play. And I stress again that our intent was never just to give an exhibition of skill. Our players were not there to be watched and applauded or to put on 'a performance', but to give and share the play when we were rehearsed enough to be ready to give it. Acting was to be the giving of a gift and the process of giving was a playing *to* and *with* the audience; both us and them sharing the same imaginative experience as givers and receivers.

A critical thing I had learned – as Tony Guthrie had done in his day – from working for radio; something germane to the business of broadcasting. In Radio all acting, all creative activity produced in the studio (the unseen stage) *was just a means to make the action of the play take place in the imagination of the audience.* This was still to a high degree – or should be – true of Stage playing. Therefore the final and most important action taking place in *any* theatre was what was happening in the imagination of the audience. We were just there to make that happen. By and large we got this into our bones and it had notable effect.

While we are on these large claims for a very small operation one should note that it was very fortunate that in any part of the auditorium the audience could all see and hear equally clearly and one did not have to think of ours as a 'thrust stage', 'in-the-round' or 'non-proscenium' theatre. It was the one place with a giving and a getting area; the latter passive on the surface but very active under the skull. So, within our theatre, I hung on to this 'broadcasting' concept of the action on stage being in the end only an artistic means to what happened in life in our Auditorium.

At the time we took over the Barn I had found an old piece of agricultural equipment – circa 1800. It turned out to have been called a 'broadcaster'. This was a seed corn container of thin and pliable wood with 8 inch sides and a bit of old iron bracketing. It was kidney-shaped in plan and when slung round the shoulders on its leather strap it sat snug round the stomach of the sower, hip-to-hip. From this custom-built container he grasped up his handfuls of seed corn and, right-hand left-hand, 'broadcast' the seed to right and left of him as he strode the furrows. It felt good to feel that rehearsal – so much of it on the old threshing floor – was the threshing out of the good grain from the chaff. Performance was the 'broadcasting': the sowing of the seed.

Back to *Wenceslas* and the underlying personal drama. Our 'playwright's workshop theatre' had not yet accomplished by this year (1980) the wrighting and the production of the two plays planned as the 'final' ones. *N for NAPOLEONE* had stepped in and made it three.

In that February 1977 I had, I find, typed a note to myself headed 'General Decisions':

> '1) To keep the Barn going until at least I have wrought the two last plays
> "The Wood For The Fire" – Wenceslas.
> "The Threshing Floor" – Boaz and Ruth.'

These plays became *Wenceslas* and *A Time of Harvest*, and these two were then seen as probably the culminating achievements of The Barn. Number 2 decision reads:–

> '2) ... and in those plays to aim at the original Truth to Love and the original Truth to Beauty.'

Under the strain, I hadn't gone either pompous or mad. I was just trying to return to the old Dedication still pinned to the backstage noticeboard.

It goes on to read; with implications obvious to you:

> '6) *Whatever happens, to give Louise more leisure and ease.*'

69

She was now doing one-eyed wonders in Admin preparation. For the *Wenceslas* event for February fill-dyke was coming up and not till August could she have the second, and now assuredly successful cataract operation. 'Of all the months I most do fear, it is the month of Februeer'. Attributed to Mary Stewart as the calendar approached her execution date at Fotheringay, I felt a dread too in my semi-Stewart Scottish bones about a Barn production now pushed into this perishing month.

But the second half of our split rehearsal period – broken by Christmas and New Year holidays – had gone well enough; and the old pause for maturing, seemed to have had effect. Louise felt fit and adventurous enough to make what was to be a surprisingly political visit to London town.

It had been our habit to have a back-stage Company Party after any Last Night and in it to give token presents of appreciation to the principals among the players and the production team. Louise was determined to have some appropriate (comically or seriously) small gifts. She consulted the Czech Consulate, looking for Czech-produced trinkets. They sent her to a Czech-run shop, which had folk art for the tourist. In the shop she cast her eye on some small items of Bohemian glass. A young assistant approached her from the backshop. And this is where the handling of a national bit of folk lore can become political dynamite. She explained that she was looking for a few inexpensive presents. They had to be Czechoslovakian – Bohemian – perhaps Bohemian glass? Why, Madam?

She explained who they were for and why Bohemian. A play? Yes – about your legendary hero-patriot. Excuse me. And the assistant went backstage and brought out of the backshop the serious faced manager; eyes summing up, the lady customer – (pleasant, intelligent-looking woman, of some substance, could be intellectual). Madame? For a Play about Wenceslas? Yes – for the players, gifts, trinkets. This Bohemian glassware... The play, Madame? Historical? Yes. Not political, Madame? Historical; these would be for after the play for... Who is the playwright, Madame? My husband. He is playwright? He writes plays. Louise never liked being pinned down by questions and normally answered one question with another. But she wanted that Bohemian glass bell and she had a history of defending refugees against political persecution. Vacel Havel, she would know through me, was still in a Prague prison, *for writing plays*. But this was England – the hell with it – it's just a play about your legendary good King Wenceslas and his page. It's only an amateur production. Ah. But not *political*? The play? No, she said. Drama is one thing politics another, he said, which doesn't give him any more credit for intelligence than he must have given to her. You wish a number of gifts? Yes, but we are not a commercial theatre and cannot afford ... He took up pieces of the glass-ware. This? and this?, this! But – And to Louise's surprise he handed to the assistant, to be wrapped up, what must have amounted to about £50 worth of glass and artware! While the assistant packaged them, the manager refused all payment. 'A gift from Czechoslovakia. But – ' and he repeated it firmly as he showed her out of the door – 'No politics.' With her provisional gift from the Czech people – or rather the Czech party – Louise came home.

For reasons having to do with the political nature of the play and my respectful distrust of the Party, there was one of the gifts I didn't let be given to anybody – a bell of Bohemian glass. It was perhaps pre-production paranoia; but the little tongue of the bell just could have been an informer; could have been bugged. If you go the whole paranoiac hog, it could be recording right now the tap of my typewriter. Because it sits over there, beyond the old octagonal table and on the old donkey-chest. Beneath our old oak beams of Grainloft it is however overseen by the innocent glass-beaded eyes of that entirely benevolent *black lamb*, mascot of *Emmanuel*. Retired from the profession, this beloved 'prop' lies peacefully draped over the oak stair rail of the steps up to my studio.

As producer of the event and in launching this play I spoke the Prologue from the centre of the up-stage gallery; spoken out under the great cross beams towards the packed audience on the benches of the auditorium, their knees blanketed against Februeer chill, The Prologue was:

'One hour before midnight on a Summer evening of *1968*, Warsaw Pact troops – moving with the co-ordination of an Imperial Army of the empires of the past – crossed the frontiers of what was once Bohemia. By breakfast of the following day the whole of Czechoslovakia was under Russian domination; and in Prague – the ancient capital of the Kings of Bohemia – the bronze statue of Wenceslas looked down on rumbling Russian tanks and stunned Czech Citizens.' Not political? 'In *928* the Imperial Army of the Franco Germanic Empire crossed the mountainous border of little independent Bohemia and, under command of Henry of Saxony, they advanced on the royal castle around which Prague grew. Once there, King Henry the German faced King Wenceslas the Bohemian, with an ultimatum; about the submission of Bohemia's independence.'

(The Howl of a Wolf is Heard)

'While the two Kings faced each other up there in the castle, Yani, a peasant, in the forest by the river down below ... '

(Light is Coming up on 'Trees' by the Deck)

YANI: *(Coming on Stage calling)* 'Samo! ... Samo! ... '

71

And we were into the action and on into the play. At the end of the play, after the murder of Wenceslas by his own brother (leader then of the party of privilege), I had to speak an Epilogue that made me feel – standing there, up near the rafters of the old Sussex Barn, as if I were out front in the world-wide battle for the spirit of the peoples:–

> 'And the ruthless, imperial invaders came again, with all the rage of the new righteousness and Bohemia was ravaged by a bloody and fruitless war. And – whether in political cynicism or by personal conviction, we don't know – Boleslav then embraced the faith of the brother he'd killed; which remained, into our day, the faith of Bohemia.'

> *(Fade to Blackout as Music Comes in – of Smetana's 'Ma Vlast' (My Country)*

One of the two 'last plays' of The Forsyths' Barn put to the test, proven good and warmly received. Only one more now – seemingly –- to go; and Louise, by no means rested, looking forward to summer and the full sight of both eyes.

With the hope to get us both out of the stresses and strains of playwrighting and production and to put to the test my ability to earn a living from my paintings, etchings and drawings, I jumped at the opportunity offered me in May of having an Exhibition in the Banking Hall of Barclay's main branch in Brighton. So – to the delight of Louise – I concentrated on this and eschewed any other Barn production till the following summer (of 1981). But, to keep faith with promises to our Friends of The Barn, a summer 1980 production was put in the able hands of he who played Henry of Saxony opposite Peter Searl's Wenceslas (and who had been playing in the Barn company since he played Joseph in the second *Emmanuel*), Michael Legat. Michael was a publisher (and is now a successful author) with much experience in production with his own first-rate amateur society. His choice of play – which we wanted to be comedy if possible – was *The Matchmaker*, which had started life modestly on the far side of the channel, as *The Merchant of Yonkers* and under the American genius of Thornton Wilder became *The Matchmaker* and finally as a fully naturalised American product, became the script for *Hello, Dolly!* If Love was a part of our dedication's commitment, well – it is a lovable if somewhat cosy play, and as well crafted as the timbers of the Barn. It was given by Michael and company a witty and fast-moving production which was a matter of delight to everyone.

This – despite the fact that the artistic autocrat of the Barn nearly ruined rehearsals by reading the riot act at a time when it looked as if we were on the way to something 'amateur', in the pejorative sense. The not improper 'kick up the backside' was administered to the players with Michael Legat present of course. But I had presumed he was with me in this. He took the whole 'rocket' as directly aimed at him. A badly handled business by the Artistic Director, who ought to have known better. I retreated in shame and confusion. He soldiered on, to deliver the goods of a most happy production; of a play he had much better understood than this playwright. Friendship has endured.

During a blazing June, following much painting in the spring, we enjoyed, and Louise had enjoyed with me, the success of the Brighton Exhibition. But, despite this proof of fair profit in the Painting, from this point on I am probably a sort of conscious criminal: the crime being to persist with the Playwrighting and all the Barn activity. The personal and professional schizophrenia of Artist/Playwright was a continuing problem for me. For I was never able *not* to believe that the plays were the deeper and the more worthwhile of the works that I had the capacity to create.

Even today – out in the now empty Barn, the worry came at me. And walking away from the deck by the bulwark where I'd gone to think – perhaps to pray – the double shafts of daylight from the two 'owl hole' windows threw a double shadow of my figure on the deck – a schizoid's shadow? But as I mounted the earth Slope, on my way to the up-stage and north exit from the playing area, the two shadows continuing ahead of me, converged. And on the wood shuttering of the back wall they became one; one image.

For a moment, in the empty building – silent except for the flutter of a dove under the high eaves outside – it came to me that, in that all-arts wonderful medium which Theatre *is*, the Playwright *and* the Artist had worked as one; and both talents been used. Rather late anyway to be only Artist for her sake. But for Love's sake? Well, let's leave this perpetual perplexity and continue the story.

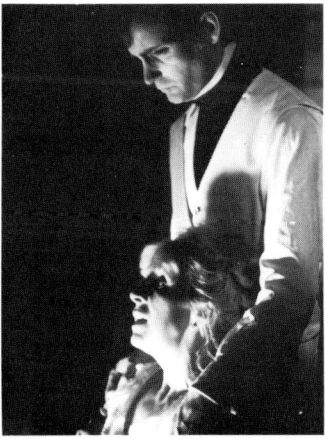

Anne Graham-Evans and Geoffrey Robertson
as Josephine and Napoleon in *N for Napoleone.*

73

The setting for *The Matchmaker*.

CHAPTER SEVEN

By Christmas 1981 the second cataract operation having been the success we hoped for, Louise had 'perfect sight'. With this, as I have indicated, came that marvellous restoration of apparently perfect health. We had however no temptation to go back on what we had already announced to all the Friends of The Barn, and Company: that in future we could not undertake to produce more than one major Drama event in any year. I had only a year to go to 70; and Louise was five years ahead of me. She had come through a pentathlon of medical trials and I was having no fun at all with arthritis. The question of running the Barn by others outside had been debated over and over again but with no good solution that would either meet the financial needs of our old age, the commitments of the Dedication, or the legal constrictions on the property too complex to consider here.

From now on there would be no levy of the perennial £2 from Friends of The Barn. The 'box-office' takings of our two collection baskets were to see us through. The one play for 1981 would be *A Time of Harvest* – the Ruth play. The Policy Group had supported me; not yet Louise. But it was a suitably summer play. As *The Threshing Floor* I had put a treatment for this forward to BBC Radio Drama, but there had been no response. (We were months into production with the Barn play, when the BBC suddenly said they *did* want to do it!) In this case the radio play came after, and only benefited by the experience of, the stage play.

With apparent good health for Louise and some pressure off us both, I found myself in the state of writing two plays at the same time; each at different degrees of development. Because while the Ruth play was in actual writing I was daily commuting to London and the British Museum Library spending blissful days in researching the subject of the new play. This was a play on the last days of the life of José Rizal, the great patriot of the Filipino people. As Rizal himself, while in exile in Britain, had spent many months of research in the blessed calm of the Library, it was rich in material related to him and the Philippines. I recall coming out for a breather to stretch my legs and stand on the steps of that famous and monumental portico. 'Dear God,' I know I muttered, 'how lucky I am to have, for the moment, the means to work on a new play whose subject is thrillingly meaningful to me; and which *could* be my best work.' Due tribute to the Arts Council encouragement. A grant from them now covered the completion of this work; and the subject had the full approval of Louise, who on reading it reckoned it *was* my best play.

This was winter work. We had committed ourselves to a scratch programme for *Music in May* – to keep touch with our faithful Friends of The Barn – but we weren't happy, nor were any of the Company, about the Barn Theatre being deserted, being 'dark', at Christmas. In order, therefore, to keep fidelity with the Festive Spirit, several of the Company undertook to organise a Company Christmas Party: Company to be in Dickensian dress! The steamy scent of hot punch once again drifted up to the old roof timbers. The whole atmosphere was redolent of the Dickens Dingley Dell Christmas Party; with a bill of entertainment delivered by the more irrepressible members of the acting company. This *was* a Merry Christmas for the Barn and all of us.

Music in May was all happiness too; and the be-ribboned maypole which all the children loved was lifted out of its socket in the Barn green and put away; for the last time. The Ruth play was completed and called *A Time of Harvest*. It would be presented at a time when the landscape of the Barn had the barley harvest going into golden ripeness in all the fields around. Summer rehearsals were always great creative fun in and around the Barn: with players not on-stage relaxed in camp chairs set about the grassy yards, thinking, studying going over lines with their mates or just resting – not 'resting' – the big doors wide to the warm air. Start of rehearsals was Easter time.

In the sessions of dream-through and scheming of the action of the play there seemed to be little need to alter greatly the basic stagings and stairs etc. But the 'new recruit' the Balcony had to be taken out and parked in the yard. This left playing space where its legs had sat; dancing space too. Another, and old element, came in – the Ramp – leading down the Slope to the threshing floor. As once it was decided 'here we'll bury the old year' I could say, 'Here' – on ramp, near a heap of threshed grain – 'Ruth will,' as Bible says, 'lie down at Boaz's feet.' Fully addressed on this Slope towards the raked auditorium, the supposed biblical seduction should begin (and Louise begin to suspect me of some concessions to soft pornography and the permissive society). Little did she know that this was not Barn inches away from where, in *Emmanuel*, our humble Mary had prayed by the bale of hay, 'As Ruth in this same Bethlehem laid down her body at Boaz's feet, I lay my body in this sweet straw. Teach me Lord how . . . ' etc. and that my character, Ruth, was of the same metal. Louise in her passionate defence of the privacy of sexual passion was still threatening not to type a scene she still hadn't even seen! Good comedy. Great days. Sunny days too.

One requisite of the basic setting was that there be space for a dance – a solo dance. This was to be a central climax of the play, happening at the time of the Judean harvest feast. It would be danced by my shy and poor gleaner refugee – Ruth the young Moabite – desert dweller – Arab if you like. For I still saw the play, with its main protagonists a refugee Moabite and a rich Bethlehem Jew, as being prototype in its pattern, of the refugee problem in the Arab/Israeli context of today, and brought into focus in antagonistic households, viz Naomi, the returned Jewish refugee, and Boaz, the land owning Bethlehemite. It was also a love drama which unlike Romeo and Juliet does not end in death but in marriage and birth; birth of a son called Obed, who begat Jesse, who begat David, whose house begat the Joseph who leads us back to that later Bethlehem again, the begetting of Jesus and all our beginnings in the Judo-Christian story.

In the dreaming and scheming I even brought back to this play that original vital, though inanimate, character from 'the hills above Bethlehem' now draped over the stair rails of my studio – the prop Black Lamb from *Emmanuel*. His dramatic purpose in this case was too complex to explain here. But the propriety of his casting as a lamb brought back to Bethlehem was unquestionable; both in point of talent and ethnic considerations too.

It was in the casting of the part of Ruth that something quite surprising happened: surprising *and* fortunate. The character had of course to be young. I had imagined her with a grace of native movement related to the tent-dwellers of the desert; those women who might carry water pitchers on their heads with ease and grace a long way from the well. She should also suggest a non-occidental obedience with the modesty of say the better sort of girl of Bedouin society. And for that critical scene she had to carry that grace into a short but exotic (Moabite) dance; exotic to on-stage Bethlehem and its Jews.

Perhaps you can remember how, two years before, we brought the dancers into the Chekhov production. I then *had* glimpsed the sort of physical grace I was now looking for, in one girl. She had been fair. I wanted a dark girl but she had danced well, there *was* an 'exotic' look about her, and her name, Noriani. I couldn't, however, know if she could act. I went over to her dance school and, by courtesy of the ever co-operative dance teacher, Drusilla, who runs the school, I had an interview with this girl, a senior student.

I said how I admired her dancing. Was she at all interested in developing her acting skills? Yes. From the beginning the whole response was biblical in its modesty. Her Yeah being gently Yeah and her Nay being quietly Nay. Would she take the play away and read it so that we could have some sort of audition later? Yes. The story, I pointed out, would be familiar enough to her – being basically the story of Ruth, in the Bible. In the Bible? Yes. She looked mildly embarrassed. Why? The Bible isn't familiar to me. You see, I am a

Muslim. I couldn't believe my ears! What better than my Ruth should be Muslim for Moabite and a stranger by belief to our Christian Bethlehemites of the Barn? She took the play away and I prayed. She seemed *so* right. And if there could be red-headed Jews why couldn't there be albino Arabs?

She read the play. She wanted to do it. She could act, so – a local Muslim, of part Malaysian parentage, played the part; and with a discipline and sort of modesty in her cultural bones one could hardly have found in a local English girl. Even an element of over carefulness with her speech helped to suggest her on-stage foreignness in contrast to the other characters. Her dancing was superb. And Noriani bemused and enamoured more than Bethlehem's Boaz.

Summer in its sunnier days was, as I've said, bliss at the Barn. And often, as you know, props and parts of the setting came from very local resources. Around the sort of old farm homestead such as ours there collects, in the buildings and the yards, flotsam and jetsam of the tides of time: weathered old wooden artifacts; sculptural pieces of oak as grey and fine as the wood on the seashore groin; old oak farm equipment; chains, ropes, cartwheels and their iron tyres, blocks and tackle etc.

In the way that a tribal African village might draw only on plants and things that were part of their natural environment to provide for festival dramas' decor and costume – eg, the "beards" of the corn cob for plumes; a giant bullrush for a ceremonial staff; straw for costume skirts; shells and bones etc – in the same sort of way I and others on design have wandered the yards and hovels on the hunt for a shape, a form, a material to provide the basis for a prop in mind. I recollect how a bit of the wood and iron mechanism surviving from a pony trap, together with lengths of old rope and a big block and tackle, served to suggest the stuff of a Boston ropewalk in *Lobsterback*! How a 'time-worn torso' of oak lying in the wood shed became the upright of the ancient whipping post in *The Other Heart* and farmyard chains finished the effect; how old sacks, a horn corn measure and cart wheels created the right atmosphere for Scene One of *The Matchmaker*.

Very locally, getting the 'several sheaves of ripe barley' needed for our festival scene was art work made pure pleasure. I got the permission again of our ever co-operative local Duaz – Eric Norris, the landowner of the fields around – and, with an old but well sharpened scythe, Forsyth went out to mow. For one sun-drenched moment of utter delight I can remember standing there amid the field of non-alien corn, and blessing my old father for having brought up the Ruth story again. The barley heads were deep gold and the stalks and leaf a pale straw with streaks of rust.

I scythed in the sun till I had laid low the makings of about seven thick golden sheaves of barley. Taking them in to the open North hovel and with the sun pouring in on us, while some curious white doves watched to see if this meant extra grain for them, I bound the seven sheaves with raffia; except for one which I bound with red ribbon. This had to be easily identified on-stage as the ritual First Sheaf of the Field. If this was the Theatre Arts at work this was work made bliss. God pity the poor pallid prop trogs working then in London town, in the concrete corridors of the National Theatre!

In our setting and lighting for this play the old Barn glowed as golden as if it were back in its original use: threshing the chaff from the good grain, for the good of the belly. This, we hoped was a threshing for the good of the soul. Except for two scaring incidents, one in rehearsal and one just off-stage during performance, most of us involved recall the rehearsals and performances of this play as pure summer pleasure.

We were 'at work' in the Barn with doors wide, sat in camp-chairs or spread on the grass; mind on the script, eyes on blue sky, with creaming clouds which had cleared the Downs and originated somewhere South-West away over the deeper blue of the English Channel. Then came *The Scare*. During rehearsals we had the sudden news that our dear and unique Moabite girl had been rushed to a Brighton hospital with acute appendicitis! Not only did this mean frantic rescheduling of rehearsals but how soon dare one dance on Boaz' threshing floor after being stitched up? With a lot of hope, and a very piece-meal month of rehearsals in no chronological order at all, we held the place she was determined to fill. At a rather late date, with no lack of guts (appendix excepted!), she got back, we had Dress Rehearsal, dance rehearsals, extra rehearsals and into the First Night in full strength.

The second scare also seemed as if Allah was not entirely on our side. It was in performance and immediately prior to our key dance on the threshing floor – Ruth's solo. Just before her entry another woman harvester in the script, 'the worse for wine' had to cast a plate or platter out towards the off-stage imagined field's edge. This was through the down-stage left entrance, into the 'Henhouse'. I had, inadvisably, insisted on a heavy bronze plate which we possessed as the best looking plate for (near Bronze Age) period and style. The actress who had to chuck it out chucked it out all right on cue, but with a hatred she had acquired for its weight. Ruth was off-stage waiting to make her entry. The bronze plate went out like a school sports day discus – with verve plus wobble but little sense of direction. No! It didn't hit our Moabite slap where the desert-tanned belly lies bare; appendix side. It fell 'to earth' but as some alert and concerned player, (who also hated that damn plate) stooped quickly to pick it up, Ruth stooped down to . . . Aow! plate edge met head. A wide cut – as if the surgeon had gone to work again in the wrong anatomical location – began to ooze blood.

I saw none of this off-stage drama in the Henhouse. I was 'out front' in my seat by the exit checking how the performance was going. Going very well it was, up to this rather favourite moment of mine – the dance. Ruth's entrance seemed delayed. (There was no great pause, thanks to superb backstage presence of mind among players and stage management.) The reed-pipe music was not broken but it was repeated. Then, fluently she made her entrance, all Bedouin grace. The dance began. The dance was *beautiful*. But I, as director, was annoyed that the splendid coin-trimmed head-dress which willing hands had worked on so hard to create so that it would sit beautifully on her tresses and veil, was now set askew. Rather 'amateur' lack of attention to detail, I thought. Then I saw what might have been blood appearing near where the coins hung and jangled on the calm Moabite brow. The dancing continued perfectly, but I slipped away, and backstage I had the off-stage emergency breathlessly explained to me. I cursed the bronze plate, cursed myself for insisting on it and blessed everybody, above all our Ruth, for 'devotion to duty far in excess of the normal requirements of the service'. The cut was not at all so bad as feared and Muslim stoicism made no complaint.

The play played to enthusiastic houses most of whose members seemed starry-eyed as they emerged. They put very adequate thank-offerings in the players' 'plate' (the collecting baskets) and as they made their way through the summer evening to their parked cars in Pax's paddock, the adjective most commonly in the air as they hailed Louise, or greeted any of us on the way, was 'superb'. On other occasions we had had 'wonderful', 'great', 'best ever' but 'superb'? That was a new one – very complimentary too, to players, production team and all.

But, in the afterglow of the success this meant to us all, let me tell you how I received, very personally, the most beautiful backhanded compliment of my entire life. I have already indicated that my very private, toughly practical and deeply passionate 'partner in life' (as my great grandad, the blacksmith, called *his* wife) had opposed the writing – and the production – of this play. Now she had seen a standing ovation and, after gusts of applause for the whole cast, there had been a call, not heard in the Barn before, of 'Author! Author!' Any sort of too personal 'curtain call' we had always avoided in the Barn: a bit too near the exhibitionism I had preached against, and certainly shouldn't practice. So I shied off going on-stage and let the call die down. It was sufficient that when the audience had drifted away and driven off there remained that echo of a very satisfactory polyphony of 'superb', 'best ever', 'superb' . . .

It was now all quiet. The last of the company's cars could be heard bumping away up the lane towards the main road. We were alone in our suddenly deserted homestead; a lot tired but not a little happy, to be basking in the afterglow of a real success. We were 'shutting up shop'. As usual, I was 'last to leave the ship' – checking that nothing had been left behind on the empty tiers of the auditorium, that all lights were switched off, etc. I shut the Barn up and opened up the gate from Pax's pen to release him on to his full range of grazing again, which had been the car park.

Clipboard, with its 'Order of the Day', under one arm I went to join Louise, who was now standing in the open on the sunset side of the Barn, thoughtful, waiting for me. The sun was almost down. It was the afterglow the Scots would call the gloaming; that lovely glow of light and warmth, so dispersed that it seems to be a luminous quality not just of light and air but of the whole atmosphere. This was 'superb' too. And as she took my arm and we both turned to move towards the house, Louise – who, remember, had opposed the play, till she saw it work quite beautifully – checked and turned. And I, my arm linked into hers, had to stop too. She then looked up, smiled wickedly and said to me the immortal words, 'You *are* a stubborn bugger, aren't you?'

The truest, most complimentary understatement I've ever had, from anybody. The night then became utter marital bliss. 'Utter', because, standing there and right on cue to our kiss, we heard one of the most welcome sounds in the world to us. It was a 'miaow!'. Kate had come back! Kate had been 'missing presumed dead'. Kate was the third of our marvellous cats (a ginger she, and so a precious rarity in even that).

The greatest hedgerow hunter of the three she could – in the summer – disappear for days at a time, and 'live on the land', sometimes 3 to 4 days – mostly on fresh rabbit! But by this night she had been away *eleven* nights and days. We had therefore begun to accept that she was 'missing, presumed dead'. (Some illicit trap, poison or speeding car.) And, as we turned at the familiar miaow, there she was, trotting down the barnyard, tail erect, lithe as a little tiger, but belly aswing with less fortunate bunny. How fortunate for us that, in that glowing gloaming, she could race up ahead of us to the cat door as we all three went up the steps where the periwinkle strays and into Grainloft and home. There are unusual domestic benefits – whatever the penalty – of having your theatre in your own backyard.

The Barnyard Gate – 1981
(And "Grainlett")

James Forsyth

CHAPTER EIGHT

A letter sent out to The Friends of The Barn, besides reporting the very satisfactory reactions to *A Time of Harvest*, said, ' . . . the Barn is now in its 10th year.' (I must have dated its theatrical life from *before* the stroke of midnight 71) 'I had always considered that it should not continue beyond seven years' and 'in recent years Louise's health has been under severe strain. Though remarkably fit now it is most unwise to continue indefinitely.' We stated that we would therefore complete this year 1981 'as planned' but from then on there would be no regular programme throughout the year – 'only isolated special drama productions' for special reasons and of special plays.

By the Autumn we realised the wisdom of this. Louise was *not* so fit as we had thought. The cancer had spread. She was having to undergo deep-ray treatment, but was responding well. Another letter went out to the Friends of The Barn.

23rd November 1981

Dear Friends of The Barn

This letter is to let you know, well ahead of the event, of the next Barn production, so that you can arrange to be present.

Because it is to be a MAJOR DRAMA PRODUCTION and it will be IN THE SUMMER – in fact in the third week of July 1982.

There will naturally be some disappointment that we have not been able to produce the Christmas play *Emmanuel* this year, as had been hoped. But this is simply a postponement and for a positively good reason. We had always said that when the time came for the Barn to cease to be a Theatre, we would end as we began, by performing *Emmanuel* at Christmas. We had some reason to fear that this year 1981 might, in fact, be the last and that the greatly appreciated *A Time of Harvest* would be the culminating drama production. That is not now so. The ardent pleas of so many Friends that we should continue have been responsible for our present decision to go ahead with a major drama production in 1982.

So, will all Friends of The Barn please make a note now of the date of the 1982 Production:

Third week of July (probably seven performances with final performance on Sunday 25th July)

and then let us have our usual "Full Houses" of appreciative Friends (and Friends of Friends); because, now that we have given up subscriptions, *all* expenses will have to be met by the theatre audience collections, which will then be the full measure of your support.

WITH EVERY GOOD WISH FOR A VERY HAPPY AND PEACEFUL CHRISTMAS TO YOU AND YOURS,

James and Louise

83

Louise being by nature a fighter and me an optimist, we went ahead but did not really know that we were proceeding on very shaky ground. We again had a heart-warming Company Party in the Barn at Christmas. We considered inviting not just the Company but all The Friends. However, that would have needed several party nights to accommodate the Friends, who officially now numbered approximately 900 (not counting children and close family).

The Summer production however was the choice of Louise. The play *would* be a 'special play' and for 'a special reason'. She chose *The Other Heart*. This play which I wrote in 1951 was first produced in the Old Vic Theatre (in 1952, two years after I had left the Old Vic Company). It was taken there by Irene Worth, who had heard the radio version which the BBC 3rd Programme did when nobody else would risk my work. She became interested in the part of Catherine when she was invited to join the Vic Company by my old friend and mentor, Tyrone Guthrie, and made it a condition that one of the parts she could play would be Catherine de Vausselles in *The Other Heart*. Guthrie, in command at the Old Vic at the time, agreed.

It was at this time that my pre-war marriage was in ruins. My sister, who had worked with her during the war, told Louise about her brother's play. Louise went along, unknown to me. She fell, of course, for the young Alan Badel, playing Villon, but she found herself moved beyond reason by the writing of the wrighter of the piece. This had then no consequence. There was no meeting of us two – till after my divorce. We first met because we were godparents at the family christening of my sister's second child. Yet one could say that, at a fairly profound level of other hearts, this particular play had brought us together. That production was in 1952.

Now, in this Winter of 1981, we were made aware that the Old Vic, my Alma Mater, where I had served my apprenticeship to the Theatre Arts, was closing down. Sadly, on December 3rd there was to be a sale of their theatrical wardrobe. That equally famous London institution, Christie's, had been brought in to conduct the public auction. It was bound to be a rather big and sentimental theatrical event. We decided to be there.

The Sale on December 3rd *was* a big theatrical occasion and inevitably 'played to a full house', with Christie's auctioneer the principal player. (Most auctioneers may well be frustrated actors.) He was perched in his 'pulpit', downstage right, hammer poised, bright of eye and, with no respect for the sadness of the occasion, wickedly enjoying the sort of joking rapport of a Frankie Howerd with a Palladium audience.

Sentiment shot all prices up to an inflationary high, quite beyond our reach, so we bought no memento. But the main purpose of our visit was more than fulfilled: to be together where we had first been brought together in spirit.

We walked the Vic stage together, where I had originally trod the boards working out the action of *The Other Heart*, which was in the final year I was 'playwright in residence' there. This time it was a question of pushing our way through rack after rack of costumes on stage and rummaging in skip after skip of props backstage. For the auction, when we had to be seated in the stalls, we tried to identify the seat where Louise had sat in 1952, and she sat in it now, possibly imagining the process of the play on stage and how it had affected her then. (The last scene's lines of Old William Villon, at the news of the death of Francois, 'This should be no surprise to me. But . . . one stumbles on the depths of love suddenly.' These were to haunt me then; and later.) At the moment it was all nostalgia for me. I had sat in most of these stall seats. I had walked the auditorium when no seats were there at all, the gallery was unsafe to use, and the theatre not yet opened to the public, because of bomb damage during the War. A memory special to *The Other Heart* came back to me because the play was in mind.

In 1949, though the theatre could not be open for public performance, a semi-private performance was taking place. And, for this playwright, then young in the art and craft of the business, it was playwrights' workshop theatre. The students of The Old Vic School (under Michel Saint-Denis, my other mentor in the Theatre Arts) were giving their end-of-term show; and to an invited audience, of theatre personalities – critics, agents etc. One of these plays being presented was a version of the legend of Penthesilea written by me and worked on closely with Michel, on the ideas side, and with the woman now his widow, Suria Magito working on the side of choreography. Much of the play's statement was in movement terms, but all arts were involved; as in this – my apprenticeship – I got my taste for total theatre.

The Dress Circle, though unlit then, must, as I remember it, have been safe to use. Because before, or after, the performance I recall recognising standing up there in the dim light, Alec Guinness. And, in my inexpert version of a stage whisper, I called up to him, 'writing a new play . . . on Francois Villon!'. We had earlier been in correspondence about my pre-war plays, written at the time he was taken into the wartime Navy and I into the Infantry. Hearing of the Villon play and knowing my struggle to survive (on £7 per half week from the Old Vic and £7 from a job of book illustration) Alec arranged, with great generosity, to let me have £100 (1946 pounds) in order to continue, concentrate upon and complete the play: which I did, calling it *The Other Heart*.

If I go on about this particular play, it's because it is critical to the climax of the Barn story.

It was the second serious frustration of the many frustrations in my career, that Alec Guinness was not able at the time of the completion of the play to take it into production and play Francois. For, one evening in Chiswick – after a reading of the whole play – he, who was to me *the* emergent star of post-war theatre, where I was a mere beginner – Alec Guinness pronounced on the play – with all the assumed divine right of us young survivors, who had just saved the World and were now about to save the Theatre, 'the greatest love play since Romeo and Juliet'.

To me, this was the Theatre itself speaking. Fame was round the corner and fortune inevitable. Poor me! And now, 1982, 'Poor Old Vic!!' – that Yorick of my instruction when I was so young in Theatre. My memory went back, embarrassingly, to the long and self-important Curtain Call speech I made on that 1952 famous First Night in response to the 'Author' call. First Nights regularly render playwrights 'temporarily insane'.

From the Auction Louise and I went home to Sussex empty-handed but hand-in-hand in that other state of blessed insanity that can make two somewhat mature lovers behave as if *they* were Romeo and Juliet.

With hospital visits continuing to yield reports which raised no special alarm and with the dropping of any Winter production in the barn making life easier for us, we went on with other work and at Christmas held a happy Company Party again.

But in February – that traditionally dreary month – nagging worries began to get at me. There was a minor amount of pain in her hip. And, in the known context, any pain assumes major cause for concern. The Doctor ordered an X-Ray; and from the results of that a 'bone scan'. Somehow the report on that came to us both ambiguously; probably because our attention at the time was riddled with anxiety. But the gentle ontologist did quietly say that there was some general spread of the cancer. The ominous phrase to me was in her clear, and again gentle, answer to my question about what best to do: 'Take holidays,' she said. Louise obviously heard this, but to her this meant defeat; and she was a fighter. Anyway, this was one person's opinion. In any case, surely, I thought we must now cancel the Summer production and . . . No! She wouldn't have it. And this I could see would be a clear sign of giving up – of throwing in the sponge. But, I argued, this was not a new play or one needing testing or re-writing. As a 'playwright's workshop' production it wouldn't be proving anything. I had already in recent years happily directed it in that other blessed wooden theatre the Tufts Arena in Massachusetts (where *Lobsterback!* had its U.S.A. premier). I personally had no heart at this time for *The Other Heart*.

But this had been her special choice of a special play, and her choice was to go on. It was her favourite play. Was the published version not dedicated to her and my son Richard? Yes. We'd take holidays all right, but *after* the play, after July. This was very much the soldier's daughter she was; who, while spiritedly 'beefing' about having to wear boots whose squeak shamed her girlish pride, yet would parade with them polished to a higher sheen than any Army requirements and then painfully march with the family all the way to the Baptist chapel.

She now even fought the gentle ontologist, went over the head of that wise and excellent lady, and, calling up the reinforcements of her remaining savings, paid for the (sadly ineffective) services of a local big gun in neuro-surgery; simply to find a way to defeat the pain, now acute in the arm. By May – with the play cast and the rehearsals begun (and with a company not privy to what you presently know) we began, separately, to sense a sort of despair.

We kept everything going, but now I wrote a letter to the consultant surgeon who had performed the original operation – the mastectomy. In him I knew Louise to have total confidence. We went to see him, in Brighton. He immediately and gravely reported to me – and this privately – 'a massive recurrence . . . She won't get better . . . but we can treat and hold it for a time.' These are the sorts of occasion when one's whole world begins to crumble; and nothing is sure, even who should share or not share in the frightening news. He had not told her. I now began *not* to accept the finality. As Louise fought the pain, I fought the idea. After all, one knew that the whole amazing business of being alive at all was a miracle of creation. I didn't believe, any more than she, in 'miracle cures', but did believe that day to day 'ordinary life' was of the stuff of miracles; and not of our making. He hadn't told her and from me Louise, the fighter, was not to know other than that the enemy had gained ground and that the fight would not be an easy one. But we were both in it, fighting, and so was he, her greatly respected consultant – who had said, 'Why didn't you come sooner?' He put her on a new drug.

And the apparently miraculous began to happen. The improvement was so apparent. 'A remarkable remission has taken place,' were the consultant's words. Well – everything took on a new lease of life. Louise, still enjoying perfect sight, and now a new hope, even joined her great chums – the costume ladies. This time the local artist Rosalie Sinclair, who had designed in the past the splendid banners for *Adelaise*, produced a fine set of well-researched costume designs. Of these Louise chose to make her personal responsibility the costume for Old William Villon; and so for me.

That last statement needs clarification. Despite some tactfully not too evident consternation in the cast, I had decided to play the part of Francois Villon's old uncle, cleric and guardian, whose care for his outrageous young genius of a ward drove him, in my play, out of his mind.

I certainly had all of the mental anguish available to qualify, though both playing in and producing a play is seldom good sense. What had happened was that the experienced player (local teacher and Shakespearean scholar too) whom I had first cast for the part, came under threat of an operation, now timed to coincide with the time of performance. The original Barn players knew that I could play the part with fair competence. I had occasionally played a supporting part – as all playwrights should do – to keep in touch with that prime art of all the arts of Theatre. Also, this being our 'last production' (already printed in the invitations) it would be my last opportunity to play in the Barn. I had the age and experience to make the part very meaningful. But had I the heart to carry it through?

Old William Villon's part involved only brief appearances in certain scenes; except the last. This was critically important. I could therefore be most of the time on duty off-stage in my normal capacity of 'orchestrator' of the whole event and of the playing team. Little could or should be expected of Louise beyond the making of my costume. But that last scene was, both privately and professionally, more critical than I had guessed it to be; even with many hard-working extra rehearsals with Francois – the other player fully involved. It wasn't that the scene was a difficult one to play. The two of us – Geoffrey Robertson and I – loved it. The danger was that the substance of the scene, about Death and Love, was rather near the bone for me – thinking about Louise.

There had been a technical problem too, about the setting for the scene. But the solution for that became something dramatically spectacular. The action of that scene is roughly this: Old William, worried to death about the disappearance of Francois into the criminal underworld of the League of Beggars, is sent, by appointment of the King, to a village outside Paris. There he will be magistrate, in charge of his own gallows tree. His appointment is part of the royal campaign to restore a Rule of Law dear to his own heart. But his duty will be ruthlessly to string up any vagrant coming his way – any of the human flotsam and jetsam abroad in the countrywide crime wave of which the League of Beggars is part. Knowing that his Francois is such a vagrant so adrift, a nightmare plagues the old man: that Francois *could* drift his way, and 'the dreadful eventuality' arrive that *he* must hang his beloved nephew. It is this unhinges the old man's mind. And Francois *does* drift into his village. In rags, rotten with a then 'terminal illness', he is so changed as to be unrecognizable. But with the last of his strength he is seeking out the one person from whom he can expect compassion and forgiveness, and refuge – his guardian Old William.

At curfew, the old man comes across him on the village green, where the new gibbet stands. He sees him only as another vagrant, and he tries to drive him away. But as the old man cannot recognize him and rambles on about the 'dreadful eventuality', Francois sees that Old William is no longer sane. And, as a last act of contrition, he chooses to see that this is his doing, his responsibility. So, he tells the old man that he knows his Francois to be already dead; thus taking away from the old man the nightmare of the 'dreadful eventuality'. Old William then – in his magisterial robes – goes, shocked, saddened, but with peace of mind. And Francois, near the end of all his strength anyway, goes alone to the ladder leading up to where the noose on the new gibbet has been hung. There he proceeds to make the final effort which will put into effect the death he had already described, when he told his old uncle that Francois was '... hanged ... one sunset ... on a country gibbet.' With hardly the strength in him to mount one rung, he goes, rung by painful rung, up the long ladder left leaning on the gibbet by the carpenters who had erected it.

I think most of our audience were genuinely afraid that he might do it. In fact with the effort to reach the top rungs from which he could reach the noose, Francois' heart gives out and he slithers back down and into the shadows at the foot of the ladder – dead.

While the old village watchman, ringing his handbell, traverses the stage in the fading sunset light, he notices nothing as he gives his curfew call of 'Cover your fires! ... Cover your fires! ...'

That may give you some idea – though probably an over-melodramatic one – of the scene; certainly of its physical requirements in setting. Sunset lighting, token trees and the dialogue of the carpenters fixing the noose on the new gibbet would take one to 'the village green at Malay-le-Roi'. But the gibbet itself? ... At the Old Vic and in the Arena Theatre in the U.S.A. 'the gibbet' was some unseen construction off-stage which threw a gibbet's shadow on-stage. And all we saw was the foot of the ladder as it slanted up and away, as it were, 'into the wings'. No wings in the Barn! So! ... How to do it?

In my lone Dreaming and Scheming sessions in the Barn I was stumped for a solution, until my eye informed my puzzled brain that there above me, in the ancient support structure of the building, was *the shape* of a gibbet. This was formed by one of the great oak support timbers, as the upright of a gibbet, and the crossbeam which it supported, as the arm of the gibbet. The flat oak brace which ran between the two and across the right-angle they made, completed the shape. This particular great oak upright ran up from the end of the

Bulwark. And if one could forget that the roof beam it supported ran on beyond the brace to arch across the width of the Barn?...Or perhaps one could isolate the gibbet shape by limewashing the beam for a foot or two beyond the brace, and the brace itself, and down the upright... In fact all we eventually had to do was hang the horribly professional hangman's noose that David had made about five feet out from the upright on the beam, and then train a baby spot on it, and to the audience it suggested 'gibbet'. (David Stredwick – senior member of our stage crew – was a local scoutmaster, and expert on knots, nooses etc.) But, the ladder? – what about that? The crossbeam was about eighteen feet up.

Well, we had a ladder. It had been part of the farm equipment since the days before we took the Barn over. I knew that it could reach right up to the queen posts above the big roof beams, because for the first *Emmanuel* it was up there that we fixed the highest spotlight in the house, and, with a blue 'gel', made it 'the star above Bethlehem'. The ladder was still sound and all Simon (next senior member of the stage crew) and I had to do was sandpaper its sides from bottom rung to as high as Francois would go, so that when our Francois slithered down its length 'lifelessly' he didn't 'die' with fifty splinters in his palms! (In the event he would work out a technique by which he came down a sort of slap by slap, rung by rung, not touching the sides at all.) But, how were we going to be able to get that long ladder in and up to the beam in the space of a scene-change; which would ruin the rhythm and flow of play if it lasted more than a minute?

Well, we found that the big ladder could be brought in from outside *at the interval* and stowed out of sight by letting it lie behind the Bulwark, on the Deck. In the scene-change two strong and deft young men (one night it was a deft girl) walked the long ladder upright, till it lay against the beam just short of where the noose was dropped in. At its foot was a batten nailed to the Deck floor, to stop any slippage. It only took seconds to get it up into position.

Now – as the upright of this 'gibbet' was the great oak pillar which ran up from the stage-right end of the Bulwark – you can see how close this was to the audience and how that noose hung down just two feet from where the front row of the audience sat below. The ladder sloped up to the high beam at an angle more acute but parallel to the slope of our steeply stepped auditorium. So that, as Francois struggled up, rung by rung, he climbed spectacularly close to the row by row of pairs of apprehensive eyes. And as, in the dim light, he struggled up closer and closer to being in reach of that noose, the tension in the place, bit by bit, grew almost intolerable; and finally, when he lost his grip, his 'heart stopped' and he mercifully slithered down and away from a tragic end, the relief was – well – cathartic, in the classical sense.

Emotion enough in that, but on the second last night life dangerously overcharged the Art with emotion almost too much to handle.

We go back to the point when the contrite Francois has just 'broken the news' to the old man, 'Francois is dead'. Playing Old William, I gave a startled little cry; and at that point I had planned to stumble forward – to steady myself on the Bulwark, running my fingers nervously along the smooth ridges of its worn surface, and then to say the line:

'This should be no surprise to me. But . . . one stumbles on the depth of Love suddenly.'

then, for a moment, to 'break down' before quickly recovering to say, 'How . . . did he die?'

But, that night, I knew Louise to be up there in the audience, wrapped up; and probably in pain. And, on the line 'one stumbles on the depth of Love suddenly' it all hit me. The loss was not of Francois but of Louise who I knew, more than I could admit, I must lose, God knows how soon.

For the rest of that scene, moving about in a sort of nightmare in the lovely free-flowing robes she had made for me I *was* a shaken, suddenly-aged creature only just in control of what I was saying and doing. But I got through and got off stage (through that little doorway leading into the cowshed through which I had, in the beginning of it all, bellowed back into the then dark Barn,

'The year that was old is becoming new.
The Love at the heart of Creation drives through
the darkest night'.)

Blundering off, I remember muttering to Margaret Coveney, the Stage Manager in that production, as I brushed past her, 'Did something very dangerous,' (which was to let the anguish of Life too acutely relate to its stimulation in Art.) But that was the tension in the atmosphere of the last Barn production.

For the last night it was more controlled. After the interval, backstage, I asked young Hilary, one of the Stage Crew, if, when she went on to make a scene-change, she would try to identify where Louise was sitting. I knew she had somewhere squeezed into the crowded auditorium again. 'Rather far back, to the right,' the report was. Already I had told Stage Management, Props, Sound etc, that this night they would all come on stage and take their Curtain Call along with the players. 'Oh no! We don't do that. We never have.' 'Tonight you do. For this night is the last night,' I said 'and I am going to get Louise on stage too.' 'Oh, in that case . . . '

When the end came, and Francois was dead and 'Cover your fires!'

was covering not a few tears shed in the auditorium, and that curfew call drifted away off-stage, there was a moment of silence and darkness, followed by applause as loud and sustained as we'd ever known. All the Company joined the players on-stage and I went forward beyond the old Bulwark and up the steps of the Auditorium to bring down Louise. Complaining but smiling I brought her to join the cheering Company on the old threshing floor. The audience roared, the Company too. And Louise had her one and only Curtain Call in our Theatre.

At this Last Night Party, there were more tears than laughter – though that was not absent. But Theatre People – and they'd all become so – are occupationally emotional. Speeches, of course, there were, and to those who had mostly guessed but did not openly know, I identified Louise's battle, its nature and state, and how she had now to be my one care; that this *was* truly – as the play's programme had said – the last performance of The Forsyths' Barn Theatre.

In the Summer weeks after this, far from all the excitement of *The Other Heart* having done her any harm it even seemed it had done her some good. On 2nd September, prior to going on the holiday we had planned, we called what would be the final meeting of the Policy Group. The Agenda had a last item headed 'The Future'. In that, we committed ourselves now to only two things in the future: 1) 'A Reunion Party' – perhaps at Christmas – and 2) 'The Little Book of The Barn' – to be written 'sometime soon'.

At that meeting there was no Bill, the Parking, or Rosemary, the Props. A year or two before Bill had retired and they had moved away to a small but beautiful cottage high up on the side of a little valley running down towards the lovely Devon valley of the River Teign, Dartmoor at its back. It was to their cottage, on their invitation that we went for one quite idyllic week of September. The weather was like Tuscany in June – warm and sunny. Then we came home.

Many times, since that amazing morning when I had wakened in the old house to the realisation that we 'had a theatre in our backyard', there had been very different mornings when I had risen with nothing but inner panic, at all that we had landed ourselves into. And many times too when Louise had burst out 'that bloody Barn!' in the way most parents of any spirit have at sometime said 'that bloody child!' of the baby crying again at 3a.m.

Now all this winter there was no pressure, just anxiety – as I more and more became nurse and Louise more limited in what she could do. There was not even a party in the Barn at Christmas, but there was one little event which celebrated Christmas and related to the Barn. The Company gradually got to know that Louise was – rather rapidly – losing ground to the enemy. She was now fighting acute pain and was rather weak. Signs of jaundice began to show; and she could hardly leave her bed now. Life became a quietly controlled nightmare for me. Might they, please, on Christmas Eve, come to 'Grainloft' and sing carols? – 'Just for Louise?' 'Of course', I said. But I didn't tell her. In her world-weariness now she might well have said, 'Please, no.'

That evening, without telling her why, I helped her out of bed and into the living room, where she could lie in our old 'relaxator' chair, wrapped in rugs and with her feet to the warmth of the wood fire. The music she may have expected me to play did not come from the record player. It came from outside; from the Barn 'waits', singing outside the house 'Away in a manger . . . '. With her warmly at ease, but too weak to sit up, I opened the door and they came in. About seven of them stood in a half-circle around Louise, as she lay, pleased but listless, in the black leather chair – not unlike her beloved Tennyson's 'Lady of Shalott' lying in her boat or Arthur in his barge. Standing there, they gently sang another carol for her. After a celebratory glass of sherry all round, they stooped to kiss her, and one by one they went, driving off in the evening up the lane.

And really, this is the end of the story I began, about The Forsyths' Barn Theatre, and the reason why *its* good life ended. The rest is too deeply personal. But you will want to know that after the privilege and anguish of nursing her myself, as she requested and in our own home, Louise died in the early hours of the tenth of January of the New Year 1983. In the testing time of the worst anguish of my life I had to face the fact, was it true what the Barn Dedication had said?

. . . 'that love is the power at the heart of Creation' or that there was truth in the defiant cry into the dark of the Barn in 1971 that

. . . 'the love at the heart of Creation drives through the darkest night!'

Well, no human, being totally human, moves out of all doubt without a little leap into hypocrisy. But having found love in its most powerful manifestation within the worst, and most hatefully destructive, days of my life, I do believe that it is true – God help us – more than ever. And that the Arts of any sort of theatre at all can do a lot worse than to, in some way, illumine that concept.

The Forsyths' Barn Theatre,

James Hough 1977

94

EPILOGUE
(1985)

As the Friends of The Barn had been previously advised, the Barn now has begun to enter a new phase of its life: not as a theatre. The Forsyths' Barn Theatre, as perhaps befits something that could only be temporary and exemplary, becomes a matter of imagination now – a mythical theatre.

The Barn, this month begins to become a fabulous dwelling for a good family. The pangs of parting with it have, for me, long since been suffered out. But legal, family and financial responsibilities had made its sale necessary. As a theatre it could not, whoever bought it, be run from the outside. Our use of it as such had kept the lovely old building in play with a lively use. To be well dwelt in became the next best option in lively use.

We – I and the family – would not put it up for auction on the open market just to get the best price possible. We were determined to know that whoever took it over would not only have the means to but would care for it as it deserved, as a lovely dwelling in a unique peaceful location. So, it has not been put on the market but a family has come, with the means and attitude we had hoped for, to convert it to its new use; while in the granary, 'Grainloft', this artist/playwright goes on to complete his life's work as such. And beyond the Barn in Old Place now a caring and neighbourly family has already come to make what may well be a most friendly and peaceful community. All three dwellings will fall 'within the curtilage' of the sheep and the doves and the benevolent spirits of its lively term of life as theatre will, we hope continue to haunt our now mythical playhouse. The heart may miss a beat at its demise but I think there is a heartbeat to all this that is definitely not downbeat.

With love to the Friends and working companions of the Barn.

James Forsyth
Grainloft
21st November 1985

THE FORSYTHS' BARN THEATRE
(Playwright's Workshop)

RECORD OF PRODUCTIONS

1972 December   *Emmanuel* — a Christmas play by James Forsyth.

1973 May   *Music in May* — a celebration of Spring.
July   *Fifteen Strings of Money* — a classical Chinese comedy by James Forsyth.
September   *Autumn Concert* — Music arranged by Howard Blake.
December   *Emmanuel* — Second Barn Production.

1974 May   *Music in May* — including a new Quartet by Howard Blake.
July   *She Stoops to Conquer* — a comedy by Oliver Goldsmith.
October   *The First and Last Adam* — Words and Music by Scholars of Wellington College.
December   *What the Dickens!* — a play by James Forsyth based on 'The Pickwick Papers'. WORLD PREMIERE.

1975 May   *Music in May* — a new operetta *The Station* by Howard Blake. WORLD PREMIERE.
June   *Lobsterback!* — a new play by James Forsyth, commissioned for the American Bicentennial. WORLD PREMIERE.
September   *A Victorian Evening.*
December   *Emmanuel* — Third Barn Production.

1976 May   *Music in May* — The Scholars, with The New English Song Book by Howard Blake.
July   *Festival of the Four* — a cycle of plays by James Forsyth, based on the Patron Saints. WORLD PREMIERE.
December   *Christmas at Greccio* — a play by James Forsyth. WORLD PREMIERE.

1977 May   *Music in May* — for Jubilee Year.
August   *Music on a Summer Evening.*
October   *Adelaise* — a play by James Forsyth.
December   *Maypoles to Mistletoe* — a folk cycle.

1978	May	*Music in May.*
	July	*N for Napoleone* — a new play by James Forsyth. WORLD PREMIERE.
	December	*What the Dickens!* — Second Barn Production.
1979	May	*Music in May* — *The Station* — Second Barn Production
	July	*A Chekhov Quartet* — short comedies by Anton Chekhov.
1980	February	*Wenceslas* — a new play by James Forsyth. WORLD PREMIERE.
	June	*The Matchmaker* by Thornton Wilder. Directed by Michael Legat.
1981	May	*Music and Dance in May.*
	July	*A Time of Harvest* — a new play by James Forsyth. WORLD PREMIERE.
1982	July	*The Other Heart* — a play by James Forsyth.

AUDIENCE REACTIONS

"The evening my wife and I spent at "FIFTEEN STRINGS OF MONEY" was one of the most wholly enjoyable of my recent play-going life – and don't forget that I am a professional play-goer. I have, since then, frequently tried to analyse precisely why it was so. Firstly, I believe one must set high value on the social factors involved. To go to the theatre in the depths of the country, having travelled through country lanes not far from one's own home and to sit amongst friends and neighbours with whom one mingles in other contexts, is preferable and, in a curious way, seems absolutely more right than going to an over-decorated metropolitan auditorium with total strangers. It makes one realise that the relationship between cast and audience, which the commercial theatre often strives to achieve (and almost invariably fails to achieve), arises naturally in this context.

"My experience at the Barn was different from any amateur experience. Here, the remarkable achievement was in the blending of professional and amateur talent – in many ways to bring out the best in both. The future, it seems to me, must take as its starting point, this marvellous feeling of community. The mixture of amateur and professional reflects, after all, the mixture of the community itself."

Richard Imeson, BBC Script Editor
Radio (Drama) London 9.10.73

"Fabulous. I loved it at the time, and it's growing on me still. The Barn is great – the play was splendid and moving – the combination is a very powerful one . . . It is real, when so much is forced or false. Your theatre stands where many English playhouses stood when Shakespeare began . . . The Barn embodies the first principles of English drama. God speed your enterprise . . . "

John Coleby. Joint Secretary, Society of Authors
London 10.12.72

" . . . The result is something unique. To say that the two events in that lovely place and atmosphere were worth the journey from London and back is the absurdest understatement. As I have said, we are not likely ever to forget them. But if the Barn means so much to us, what must it mean to your whole neighbourhood, to all the people who help in the work, who have each something to give and now have a chance to give it, and are brought together by doing something really creative."

Jonathan Griffin, Writer & Translater
London 27.8.73

"It gives me particular pleasure to write to you outlining what my visit to the Barn Theatre has meant, and indeed my broad feelings about the pioneering that you have done for part of the country, to create a genuine Community Theatre that owes its enthusiasm not only to yourselves but to the community in which you live. I personally believe that Drama must – essentially *must* take place where the enthusiasm to perform and the enthusiasm to receive performances, exists. Surely these qualities are explicitly manifest in the Barn Theatre."

Anthony Cornish, BBC Producer
London 21.8.73

"The Barn Theatre is overwhelming – especially in respect to its sense of humanity and dedication. We, the Burnims, of course bask in its reflected glory and excitement. We wish to share it with you. Please accept this modest contribution to the project from us. It is an offering with love, admiration and gratitude." (Cheque enclosed for Fifty Dollars)

Dr. Kalman Burnim, Chairman Drama Department
Tufts University, Medford, Mass. U.S.A. 24.1.73

"In my opinion, in the Barn Theatre there are all the ingredients of something very special. The barn itself is uniquely suited to theatre of the highest order. It has spanned centuries durings its existence, and stands now with all the strength, craftsmanship and beauty with which its builders endowed it long, long ago. It has an atmosphere, in fact, of serene timelessness.

"There is the advantage, a purely practical one, of having so much in the way of buildings for use as dressing rooms, already existing. There is the secluded and lovely setting in which the barn is situated – secluded yet very accessible. Lastly there is you, James and you, Louise, with between you the professional skill and knowledge of the theatre, with friends and contacts all over theatrical circles and with the ability to cope with the business details and the down to earth practical work involved. With all these things coming together in one place, the ingredients are there for a potential "Glyndebourne in miniature".

Marjorie Hervey, Chard, Som. 19.8.73
(formerly of Highbridge Mill, Cuckfield)

"As you know, I have been indirectly associated with the theatre for many, many, years; when I was a Story Editor at Twentieth Century Fox Films and then later as a Literary Agent. I was so very impressed by the productions of EMMANUEL and FIFTEEN STRINGS OF MONEY, especially by the high standard of local talent. The whole atmosphere of your barn is so right for the training and inspiration of creative young people. Every neighbourhood needs but rarely has the chance to have such a wonderful old Barn Theatre, with two talented professionals at the helm. Haywards Heath is lucky . . . "

Cecily Ware, Theatrical Agent
London 28.8.73

"I want to say how much I have enjoyed the Barn Theatre as a member of the audience and as a small member of the production staff. To work in a barn of such age and beauty creates the proper sense of humility in performers (and audience) in a way which is often lacking in a purpose-built modern piece of concrete. The whole experience forces one back to an awareness of the roots of drama in myth and story-telling. It must be one of the most stimulating places in which to work or to watch."

Richard E. Hughes, Theatre and TV Director
London 20.8.73

"I can't begin to tell you how much I have enjoyed and been stimulated by my small part in helping to make the Forsyth Barn project establish itself. The building and its setting are so beautiful and cry out to be used to their fullest as a cultural centre for that area. The people that I met while working on FIFTEEN STRINGS OF MONEY" (he played a leading part in the production) "demonstrated such refreshingly selfless enthusiasm and dedication to the project that it cannot but succeed . . . "

Paul Seed, Professional Actor
London 11.8.73

"We injoyed the play yesterday and we would like to thank your fiends for doing this play and at school we are doing the same as you. And I like the tea your fiends made for us and I hope you have a very nice Christmas."

Simon Barrie *(aged 7)*

The foregoing represents a proportion only of the many letters received as a result of the activities in the barn during this first experimental year 1972–3.